HIGHLINE COLLEGE LIBRARY
WITHDRAWN
Highline College Library

Quickly Master the New Features of Microsoft® Office 2013

A Hands-on Approach

Editions covered:
Office Home and Student 2013
Office Home and Business 2013
Office Professional 2013
Office Professional Plus 2013
Office 365 Home Premium
Office 365 Small Business Premium
Office 365 ProPlus
Office 365 Enterprise

Debora A. Collins

D1533815

Copyright © 2012 by Certibility, LLC
1422 W. Beacon Hill Circle
Salt Lake City, UT 84123

ISBN-13: 978-1481243445
ISBN-10: 1481243446

All rights reserved. No part of this publication may be reproduced or distributed in any form or by any means, or stored in a database or retrieval system, without the prior written permission of the publisher.

Trademark Acknowledgements

Microsoft and the trademarks listed under Legal and Corporate Affairs at http://www.microsoft.com/about/legal/en/us/intellectualproperty/trademarks/en-us.aspx are registered trademarks of the Microsoft group of companies in the United States of America and other countries. All other trademarks mentioned in this publication are the property of their respective owners. Certibility is not associated with any product or vendor mentioned in this publication.

Disclaimer

In an effort to deliver this information to readers in a timely manner, this publication has been written based on Office 2013 Professional Plus RTM. There may be minor changes between the screenshots provided in this book and what the reader experiences in their edition of software.

The example company Two Tire Tours and its domain name, email addresses, logos, people, places, and events used in this publication are fictitious. No association with any real company, organization, domain name, email address, logo, person, place, or event is intended or should be inferred. The name Two Tire Tours and its domain name and email addresses are owned by Certibility, LLC.

This publication expresses the author's views and opinions. The information contained herein is provided without any express, statutory, or implied warranties. Neither the author, publisher, Microsoft Corporation nor its resellers or distributors, will be held liable for any damages caused, or alleged to be caused, either directly or indirectly, by this publication.

About the Author

Debora A. Collins is a Microsoft Certified Learning Consultant (MCLC) and a well-known educator in the Microsoft Office community.   She has an M.S. degree in Education from Brigham Young University (1985) with emphases on Curriculum Development, Instructional Methods, and Computer Science. For the past 25 years, Debbie has been immersed in classroom and remote instruction to learners of all ages within academic, government and corporate organizations. She writes curricula about a variety of Information Technologies. Included in her most recent projects has been the development of a series of preparation workshops for the Microsoft Office Specialist (MOS) certifications versions 2003 through 2013. Debbie speaks at numerous International, National, Regional, and State-level conferences where she educates audiences on the value of MOS certification while demonstrating the features of the latest version of Microsoft Office. From January, 2009 through June, 2012, Debbie authored an "Office Tips and Tricks" column for the official Microsoft trainer newsletter called the, "MCT Flash", which was distributed monthly to Microsoft instructors worldwide.

Debbie holds and keeps current a variety of IT certifications. Her most prominent Microsoft credentials include Microsoft Certified Learning Consultant (MCLC), Microsoft Certified Trainer (MCT), Microsoft Certified Systems Engineer (MCSE), and Microsoft Office Master.

She travels between two residences - a condo in Salt Lake City, Utah where she bases most of her work; and a small family farm located outside of Medford, Oregon.   In her spare time Debbie enjoys dancing, camping, traveling, genealogy, SCUBA, and playing a variety of sports.

Inquiries to schedule Debbie for speaking or teaching engagements may be emailed directly to her at dcollins@certibility.com

Acknowledgements

Many friends in both my personal and professional life encouraged me to write this book.   Thanks to all of you! I especially appreciate the time spent by Sandy DuBose and Dr. Randall Thunell who spent countless hours proof-reading and editing for me.

I also thank my tennis and volleyball buddies for taking me away from my keyboard a couple nights each week so I could maintain my sanity!

Contents

Preface

For the past seven years my students and colleagues have pressured me to share my Microsoft Office expertise by writing a book. This is my first attempt. Please bear this in mind as you read! Let me know if you find any serious flaws or have suggestions for improvement. Or, just drop me a note if you like it! I welcome your feedback. My email address is provided in the section titled, "About the Author".

I suppose you could label me an all-round educator. I'm a teacher, a trainer, a consultant, and curriculum developer. We'll see if I have any talent as an author. Whenever I teach, I always have two goals for my students: 1) that you learn something you didn't already know; and 2) you have fun while you're learning. It is my hope that you will experience both with this book. Thank you for your purchase! ☺

Enjoy!

Debora A. Collins

Chapter 1:
How to Use this Book

This chapter covers the following topics:

- ✓   Prerequisites: Who should read this book?
- ✓   Two Learning Styles - Reading vs. Doing
- ✓   Editions of Office 2013
- ✓   System Requirements
- ✓   Installing Office 2013
- ✓   Installing the Demonstration Files

This book is intended to save experienced Office users (like you) time by covering *just the new features* contained in Office 2013. This is not a publication for new users of Microsoft Office. This book assumes you are already comfortable with the Ribbon and the common functionality contained in earlier versions of Office 2007, Office 2010, or Office 2011 for Mac. By focusing on just the new features of Office 2013, it is the goal of this book to help you understand them and master these changes as quickly as possible.

To begin, let us identify what you should already know prior to using this book…

Prerequisites: Who should read this book?

To have the best learning experience from this book, you should already have the following background:

- Be familiar with "the Ribbon" user interface on a previous version of Office for either the PC or Mac.   These versions are either Office 2007 or Office 2010 for the PC, or Office 2011 for Mac.

- Be comfortable with basic use of the application (Word, Excel, etc.) presented in the chapter you are reading. This book will not teach you how to use an application. Remember, the goal of this book is simply to help you master the new features in an application.

- Be familiar with features located in the "backstage view" of recent versions of Office (i.e., the File tab).

Two Learning Styles - Reading vs. Doing

How do you prefer to learn? This book is designed for two types of learners. There are those of you who just want to receive the information as fast as possible, like drinking water from a fire hose! Then, there are those who learn best by experience, the "hands-on" approach. This book is written for both types of learners.

If you are a learner who prefers to acquire information simply by reading about it, then you should focus on the first two chapters of this book but skip installing Office 2013 and the demonstration files. The first two chapters summarize all of the changes found in Office 2013. The remaining chapters address the new features in greater detail for each specific application. You can choose to read those chapters of interest to you and skip the hands-on demonstrations. If you do this, you should be able to meet your goal of becoming acquainted with the new features of Office 2013 in a few hours. This strategy should serve as a high-level overview, saving you days of digging the information off the Internet.

On the other hand, if you prefer to learn by doing then you should read through this entire book. Read through Chapter One and make sure to install Office 2013 and the demonstration files so you can follow the hands-on exercises included in the remaining chapters. Read through Chapter Two and any chapters addressing the new features of the applications that interest you. In each of the application chapters you choose, follow along with the demonstrations for a "hands-on" experience. This learning strategy will take longer than just simply reading through the book; however, it will provide you the richest experience.

Regardless of your learning style, enjoy the journey!

Editions of Office 2013

On June 28, 2011 Microsoft introduced Office 365. It was sold as a yearly subscription and it was installed over an Internet connection; there were no DVDs or CDs. Upgrades were automatic. Customers liked it.

Office 2013 is built on the success of Office 365. Customers can buy either a traditional desktop edition of Office 2013 (a DVD, upgrades are purchased separately), or an Office 365 edition (yearly subscription). The benefit of Office 365 is that upgrades are included in the subscription and can occur multiple times in a year. This book explains cloud-based computing in Chapter Two. In this section, we examine the differences between the traditional editions and subscription editions of Office 2013.

Traditional Editions (desktop-based)

These are boxed editions of Microsoft Office, typically installed from a DVD, but can be installed over a network if a network administrator chooses to deploy that way. Next is a summary of these editions.

Office Home and Student 2013

Home users and students who need Office on only one device may purchase a desktop edition called, "Office Home and Student 2013". It includes Word, Excel, PowerPoint and OneNote. This edition allows the user to save documents online and on the local computer. As with previous versions of Office it includes patches and updates, but not version upgrades. Version upgrades must be purchased separately. Office Home and Student 2013 is the most basic edition of Office 2013.

Note: A version of this edition called Office Home & Student 2013 RT comes pre-installed on all Windows RT devices (i.e., tablets) and includes the fully featured applications Word, Excel, PowerPoint and OneNote optimized for the ARM processor. Touch features and longer battery life are enabled by default. The RT edition comes bundled with Windows RT devices and is not available for purchase as a standalone product.

Office Home and Business 2013

This edition contains everything found in Office Home and Student 2013. To support email, scheduling, contact management, to-do-lists, and other common business organizing tasks, this edition also includes Outlook. It may be installed on only one PC or Mac.

Office Professional 2013 and Office Professional Plus 2013

This edition includes everything in Office Home and Business 2013 with Access and Publisher. As with the other traditional editions, documents may be stored either online or on the local computer. Office Professional 2013 may only be installed on one PC or Mac; however, the "Plus" edition is sold under volume-licensing. "Plus" also includes InfoPath and Lync.

Subscription Editions (cloud-based)

Beginning with Office 2013, Microsoft is packaging subscription editions with hardware sold by partners. Next is a summary of these editions.

Office 365 Home Premium

Designed for household use, this edition can be installed on up to 5 PCs or Macs, and select mobile devices such as tablets. Subscribers receive Word, PowerPoint, Excel, Outlook, OneNote, Access, Publisher, and ongoing access to version upgrades and multiple languages. By default, documents are stored online on a SkyDrive (explained in Chapter Two). You may also store a local computer; however, storing online allows you to access your saved documents and personal application settings from any device at any time. When you're away from home, documents can be edited using a new Microsoft technology called "Office on Demand" where applications can be streamed to any computer for temporary use. Subscribers of this edition also get an extra 20GB of SkyDrive storage, plus 60 minutes of Skype phone calls each month to 40+ countries.

Office 365 Small Business Premium

This edition includes the same applications as Office 365 Home Premium, plus InfoPath and Lync. It is designed for businesses with 10 employees or less. Each user can install Office on up to 5 PCs or Macs, and on select mobile devices such as tablets. This edition does not include Skype; however, it provides many business-related benefits such as Exchange Online with a 25GB mailbox for each user, shared calendars, contact management, scheduling and task-list tools, 10GB of SharePoint Online storage for sharing organization documents plus 500MB of SharePoint Online workspace per user, High-Definition (HD) video conferencing hosted by Microsoft, plus business collaboration and website tools.

Table 1. Office 2013 Editions Compared

	Subscriptions		Traditional Purchases		
	Office 365 Home Premium	Office 365 Small Business Premium	Office Home & Student 2013	Office Home & Business 2013	Office Professional (Plus) 2013
Core Office Applications Word, Excel, PowerPoint, OneNote[1]	●	●	●	●	●
Email, Calendars, Tasks Outlook	●	●		●	●
Publishing, Databases Publisher, Access[2]	●	●			●
Collaboration, Forms Lync, InfoPath		●			Plus Edition only
Personalized Experience Applications, settings and documents are always accessible	●	●	●	●	●
Easy subscription Ongoing access to version upgrades and languages	●	●			
Multiple Installations Up to 5 PCs or Macs *and* select mobile devices[3]	●	●			Plus Edition only
Office on Demand Office applications are streamed to your PC[4]	●	●			
SkyDrive +20 GB Additional storage to save documents online	●				
Skype World Minutes 60 minutes of Skype calls each month to phones in 40+ countries[5]	●				

Virus/Spam Protection Shared calendars and a 25GB mailbox protected against viruses and spam		•			
Cloud Storage 10GB general storage plus 500 MB *per user* for easy access to business documents from anywhere		•			
High-Definition Videoconferencing Conduct online meetings and desktop sharing with video and audio[6]		•			
Business Collaboration and Website Tools Create websites, share documents online and stay connected to your team		•			
Number of Installations	5 PCs or Macs	5 PCs or Macs	1 PC or Mac[7]	1 PC or Mac[7]	1 PC
Licensing Model	Household	User	Device	Device	Device
MSRP (USD)	$99.99 /year	$150.00 /user/year	$139.99	$219.99	$399.99

[1] Not available on Mac
[2] PC only
[3] Smartphones and tablets added regularly. Availability of Office 365 apps varies by device. Subscription begins at Office 365 account setup.
[4] Windows 7 or Windows 8 operating system required, Internet connection required.
[5] See http://office.microsoft.com for details. Skype account required. Excludes special, premium and nongeographic numbers. Calls to mobiles are for select countries only. Skype available only in select countries.
[6] HD video camera required.
[7] PC versions 2013; Mac version 2011

Source: http://www.microsoft.com/en-us/news/download/presskits/office/docs/PlacematFS.docx

Two other editions exist: Office 365 ProPlus and Office 365 Enterprise. The first is primarily a licensing extension of Office 365 Small Business Premium. The second includes additional online services to support large enterprises. A brief description of these two editions follows.

Office 365 ProPlus

Everything in Office 365 Small Business Premium is included in this edition. The major difference is that Office 365 ProPlus allows an organization to create up to 25 user accounts. Each of these 25 users can install Office on up to 5 PCs or Macs, and on select mobile devices such as tablets.

Office 365 Enterprise

Specifically designed for large enterprises, this edition has the benefits of Office 365 ProPlus combined with online services for Exchange, SharePoint and Lync. Exchange Online provides archiving and legal hold services to manage email in the cloud. SharePoint Online manages documents across the enterprise, and Lync Online helps the organization conduct virtual meetings and collaborate across remote teams.

System Requirements

The system requirements for Office 2013 are minimal. Most computers that are successfully running either Office 2007 or Office 2010 should already meet the requirements for Office 2013. A few of the applications within Office 2013 have additional requirements. In this book, additional requirements will be identified in the chapter for that specific application.

Keep in mind the basic system requirements that follow *do not* apply to Windows RT devices (i.e., tablets). As mentioned earlier in this book, Windows RT devices come with the Office Home and Student 2013 RT edition pre-installed. This RT edition cannot be purchased separately.

The requirements described in this section pertain to the following editions of Office 2013, whether desktop-based, cloud hosted, or a hybrid of both:

- Office Home and Student 2013
- Office Home and Business 2013
- Office Professional 2013 and Office Professional Plus 2013
- Office 365 Home Premium
- Office 365 Small Business Premium
- Office 365 ProPlus
- Office 365 Enterprise

Table 2. Minimum System Requirements for Office 2013

Computer and processor	1 gigahertz (Ghz) or faster x86- or x64-bit processor with SSE2 instruction set
Memory (RAM)	1 gigabyte (GB) RAM (32 bit); 2 gigabytes (GB) RAM (64 bit)
Hard Disk[1]	3.0 gigabytes (GB) available
Display[2]	Graphics hardware acceleration requires a DirectX10 graphics card and 1024 x 576 resolution
Operating[3] **System**	Windows 7, Windows 8, Windows Server 2008 R2, or Windows Server 2012
Browser	Microsoft Internet Explorer 9 or 10, Mozilla Firefox 12, Apple Safari 5, or Google Chrome 18.
.NET version	3.5, 4.0, or 4.5
Multi-touch	A touch-enabled device is required to use any multi-touch functionality. However, all features and functionality are always available by using a keyboard, mouse, or other standard or accessible input device. Note that new touch features are optimized for use with Windows 8.
Additional requirements	Some functionality may vary, based on the system configuration. Some features may require additional or advanced hardware or server connectivity.

[1] System requirements are rounded up to the nearest 0.5 GB, to be conservative. For example, if an application's required hard disk space is 1.99 GB, Microsoft recommends 2.5 GB of disk space. Hard disk requirements are intentionally larger than the actual disk space usage of the software

[2] A graphics processor helps increase the performance of certain features, such as drawing tables in Excel 2013 or transitions, animations, and video integration in PowerPoint 2013. Use of a graphics processor with Office 2013 requires a Microsoft DirectX 10-compliant graphics processor that has 64 MB of video memory. These processors were widely available in 2007. Most computers that are available today include a graphics processor that meets or exceeds this standard. If a computer does not have a graphics processor, it can still run Office 2013.

[3] As of the writing of this book, Microsoft had not yet announced the system requirements for Macs.

Source: http://technet.microsoft.com/en-us/library/ee624351(v=office.15).aspx#Overview1

Installing Office 2013

Before you can complete the demonstration exercises in this book, you must first install one of the editions of Office 2013. All of the Office 2013

editions install quickly, requiring only a few minutes. Office 2013 is supported for both 32-bit and 64-bit client applications. Microsoft recommends that you also install Silverlight together with Office 2013 to improve the online experience; however, this is not a requirement. All editions of Office 2013 do require Windows 7 or Windows 8 as the installed operating system. Office 2013 will *not* run on Windows XP!

The cloud-based editions co-exist nicely with earlier versions of Office already installed on a computer. Microsoft has announced that the final release of all editions, desktop and cloud-based, will install side-by-side with previous versions of Office. This is a deliberate design to make deployment easier within organizations so there will be no need to disrupt users to uninstall a previous version before installing Office 2013.

If you have no interest in reading about the new technologies supporting installation, skip to the end of this section to the Step-by-Step Installation Instructions. Otherwise, put on your geek hat and continue reading...

Say Goodbye to MSI-based Installations

Microsoft has stated that the final version of Office 2013 may be deployed via the Office 365 cloud or by using traditional deployment methods; however, network administrators should note that MSI-based installations cannot take advantage of the newer, faster, cloud-based streaming technology incorporated into Office 2013. Nor can MSI-based packages support side-by-side operation with older versions of Office. Although it is technically possible to install Office 2013 by creating an MSI-based package, all previous versions of Office must first be uninstalled prior to launching the MSI-based package. As an alternative to this traditional Windows Installer method of deploying and updating Office, Microsoft encourages network administrators to instead use the Click-to-Run technology which was introduced to consumers with Office 2010.

What is Click-to-Run?

Click-to-Run is a Microsoft streaming and virtualization technology that reduces the time required to install Office. It also creates an environment that makes it possible for Office 2013 to reside side-by-side with a previous installation of Office 2010, Office 2007, or Office 2003.

Benefits of Streaming Technology

The streaming technology of Click-to-Run enables you to download and begin to use an Office product before the entire product has finished installing on your computer. One of the many benefits of Click-to-Run is that it can also be used to update Office products. Its streaming and virtualization capabilities are based on Microsoft Application Virtualization (App-V). In Office 2010, Click-to-Run was available to consumer users only, but with Office 2013, Click-to-Run also supports large enterprise deployments.

As previously mentioned, Click-to-Run is an alternative to the traditional Windows Installer (MSI-based) method of installing and updating Office. If you install Office by using MSI, you have to wait until the entire Office product is installed before you can open and start to use the product. With the streaming capabilities in Click-to-Run, you can open and begin using the product while the rest of the product is being downloaded in the background. If you attempt to use a feature in Office 2013 that is not yet installed, Click-to-Run immediately downloads and installs that feature.

Another benefit to Click-to-Run products is they are always up-to-date. This eliminates the need to apply service packs immediately after installing an Office product. By default, Click-to-Run products are configured to update automatically so users don't have to download or install updates. The Click-to-Run product seamlessly updates itself in the background. If you want to view the update status of a Click-to-Run product, it is displayed under the File tab of Office 2013.

Another benefit of Click-to-Run streaming is the Office product is not running from a server on the Internet or from a server on your local network. The Office product is installed on the local computer, so users can disconnect from the network or Internet and use the Office product as soon as its core components are downloaded. Click-to-Run streaming makes installing and updating Office 2013 quick and easy.

Benefits of Virtualization Technology

The virtualization technology of Click-to-Run operates Office 2013 in a self-contained, virtual environment on the local computer. This isolated environment provides a separate location for the Office 2013 programs and settings to run so they don't affect other applications installed on the computer. This virtualization technology allows similar Office versions, such as Excel 2013 and Excel 2010, to run side-by-side.

Even though the Office product runs in a self-contained environment, it can interact with other applications installed on the same computer. Features such as macros, in-document automation, and cross-Office product interoperability will work. Click-to-Run is also designed to allow locally-installed add-ins and dependent applications to work; however, some add-ins might misbehave or might not work at all with Click-to-Run.

Thanks to the virtualization technology of Click-to-Run, a user can test a new version of Office 2013 without having to uninstall an older Office version; however, the following are two important considerations about side-by-side Office installations:

- The earlier version already installed on the computer must be one of the following: Office 2010, Office 2007, or Office 2003.

- Versions of Office that reside side-by-side must be the same, either 32-bit or 64-bit. For example, both installations of Office must be either 32-bit, or they must both be 64-bit, they cannot be mixed.

Overall Benefits of Click-to-Run

The following are the overall benefits of Click-to-Run in Office 2013:

- Faster download and installation. The user can begin using Office 2013 before it has finished installing.

- Office products are up-to-date when installed and kept up-to-date automatically. No need to install updates manually.

- Different versions of Office products can co-exist side-by-side on the same computer.

For network administrators reading this book, know that you can also use software management tools with Click-to-Run. For example, you can use software management tools to do the following:

- Download Office product and language files to a local server, and then distribute those products and languages to users using the Microsoft System Center Configuration Manager.

- Click-to-Run and MSI versions of Office products use the same set of Group Policy settings, so standard configurations for users and computers can be enforced.

Overall, Click-to-Run is a great addition to Office 2013!

Step-by-Step Installation Instructions

The following step-by-step instructions demonstrate how easy it is to install Office 2013 using the Click-to-Run technology discussed in the previous section. If you are reading this book prior to the final release of Office 2013, these instructions will work to install the "Customer Preview" of any of the cloud-based editions. The Customer Preview is the BETA (pre-release) version of Office 2013 that Microsoft made available for public testing beginning July 16, 2012. After the final release of Office 2013, the Customer Preview editions will no longer be available, but the steps to install any of the releases should remain the same with little deviation. Let's install Office 2013!

1. Using a browser, go to **http://office.microsoft.com/**

2. Click on **Sign Up**. Create a new account. (Note: If you are currently an Office 365 subscription user, you'll need to sign up for a new Microsoft account that is different from your active Office 365 login credentials before you can test the Customer Preview).

3. After you've signed up for a Microsoft account, use your new ID to **login** to **https://login.microsoftonline.com**.

4. Click the **Download Software** shortcut and choose a trial edition.

5. Click the **Install** button. This will launch the new "Click-to-Run" installer.

6. Review the licensing agreement and click **Accept**

7. The core of Office will install within a few minutes while you watch an introductory video explaining some of the new Office features.

8. Choose a look to personalize your new Office client applications.

9. You may begin using Office while it installs in the background over the next few minutes.

Installing the Demonstration Files

This book uses a hands-on approach to help you quickly master the new features of Office 2013. Although not required, you are encouraged to complete the demonstration exercises as you read along. The demonstrations were written for a PC; however, they should also work on other devices, if you adjust accordingly (i.e., on tablets, double-tap instead of double-click, and finger-hold instead of right-click; on a Mac, hold the CTRL key + click instead of right-click).

To support the demonstrations, a set of files are provided for you. The following steps will download these files onto your computer.

1. Go to this book's website at **http://www.certibility.com**

2. On the Certibility, LLC website click the tab, **Book Support**

3. Click the icon, **Office 2013 DemoFiles.zip**

4. Choose a location on your computer to save the file, then click **OK.**

5. After the download is complete, locate the file on your computer.

6. Unzip the file. To do this on the PC, right-click the file and select **Extract All...** On the Mac, double-click the file; Tablets, finger-hold.

With these demonstration files downloaded and unzipped onto your computer, you are ready to begin learning the new features of Office 2013.

Chapter Summary

In this chapter you learned the goal of this book is to help experienced Office users master the new features of Office 2013. It was explained that this book accommodates two learning styles – reading and doing. Learners who prefer reading were instructed to focus on the first two chapters. Learners who prefer a hands-on approach were instructed to download the book's accompanying files, read the chapters of interest, and follow along with the demonstrations. It was emphasized that this book covers only the new features so readers avoid wasting time on features that existed in earlier versions of Office. This book is not for new users of Microsoft Office.

The various editions of Office 2013 were described and compared. They were categorized as either traditional (desktop-based) or subscription (cloud-based) editions. You learned that the traditional editions are: Office Home and Student 2013, Office Home and Business 2013, Office Professional 2013, and Office Professional Plus 2013. The subscription editions are Office 365 Home Premium, Office 365 Small Business Premium, Office 365 ProPlus and Office 365 Enterprise. These editions differ primarily in their number of applications, licensing, and online services. The traditional editions can still be packaged as .MSI and installed using Windows Installer; however, all of the editions can be deployed with Click-to-Run technology which speeds up installation and allows Office 2013 to reside side-by-side with previous versions of Office. All of the editions, except Office Professional 2013 and Office Professional Plus 2013 can be installed on either a PC or Mac; however, a few applications within the editions are not available for Mac. PC installations require either Windows 7 or Windows 8 as the operating system. Windows RT devices (i.e. tablets) are pre-installed with Office Home and Student 2013 RT which has been optimized for ARM devices.

Step-by-step instructions demonstrated how to install Office 2013 from a cloud-based source using Click-to-Run technology.

The chapter concluded with a set of instructions to download and unzip the files which support the demonstrations contained in this book

Chapter 2: What's New About Office 2013?

This chapter covers the following topics:

- ✓ A New Look and Feel? Yes and No
- ✓ Welcome to Cloud Computing!
- ✓ SkyDrive
- ✓ SharePoint Online
- ✓ Office Store
- ✓ A Summary of New Application Features

On July 9, 2012 Kurt DelBene, President of the Microsoft Office Division, along with Steve Ballmer, CEO of Microsoft, announced at the Microsoft Worldwide Partner Conference that Office is installed on one billion machines around the world! That's a pretty impressive number. One week later, Microsoft announced a preview of Office 2013 to the public.

What's new about Office 2013? The first thing you'll notice about Office 2013 is that it is designed to run on Windows 7 or Windows 8 PCs and tablets. Mac and Android compatibility will be available spring, 2013. Office 2013 is a shift into cloud-computing which enables document collaboration and access from anywhere and from any device. Several new features have been incorporated into this new version of Office. This chapter will provide a comprehensive overview of these changes.

A New Look and Feel? Yes and No

Does Office 2013 have a new look and feel? That depends on which operating system you are using with it. If you run Office 2013 on the

Windows 7 operating system, you won't notice much change in the appearance of Office. In fact, the environment comfortably resembles that of Office 2007, Office 2010 or Office 2011 for Mac. The color scheme will be slightly different and the Ribbon user interface "autohides" by default to allow for a larger document workspace; but at first glance, Office 2013 will not seem that different in its look and feel from previous versions.

If you run Office 2013 on Windows 8, you will see the Metro-style look and feel at initial startup. Office 2013 fits well inside Windows 8 with the applications appearing as tiles; however, it is not fully Metro. Office 2013 runs in the Desktop side of Windows 8, not the Metro side. The Start experience of Office 2013 looks similar to previous versions of Office, but it is simplified in the way recent documents and templates are offered. Once Office 2013 is launched, the inner workings look very similar to Office 2007, Office 2010 or Office 2011 for Mac. One noticeable "feel" change to Office 2013 when running on Windows 8 is Touch Mode, but most people report the touch support is disappointing on x86/x64 computing devices. The major complaint is that it is a bit clunky. The consensus seems to be that on x86/x64 computing devices Office 2013 is best operated with a keyboard and mouse.

On tablet devices, Office 2013 also runs on the Desktop side of the operating system and it has some limitations. The most obvious of these limitations when running Office 2013 on the Windows RT operating system is the lack of support for Office macros and add-ins. The trade-off is that Office 2013 optimizes touch and pen capabilities on Windows RT.

So, when addressing the question "Does Office 2013 have a new look and feel?" The answer must be "yes, if running on the Windows 8 or Windows RT operating system". The answer is "no" if running on Windows 7.

Welcome to Cloud-Computing!

The most obvious change in Office 2013 is the shift to cloud-computing. If you're not yet acquainted with the term, don't feel alone. Many people are still new to the idea. So, let's explain it....at least from Microsoft's point of view.

Understanding "the Cloud"

What exactly is this "cloud"? There are many explanations, but Wikipedia defines cloud-computing most succinctly as:

"...the use of computing resources (hardware and software) that are delivered as a service over a network (typically the Internet)."

Source: http://en.wikipedia.org/wiki/Cloud_computing

Did you catch the keyword in that definition? It's *service*. The "cloud" is a term identifying software, data storage, and other services delivered to users over a network connection, usually the Internet. Businesses have been providing these services to their employees for years using private networks. More recently, similar services are being offered to the public either free or via fee-based subscriptions. A good example of a cloud-computing service that's been around for years is web-based email. If you've ever used an email service like Hotmail, Gmail, or Yahoo! Mail then you have already experienced cloud-computing! It just didn't have that label years ago when you started using the service.

The sources providing these services may be physically housed anywhere in the world and typically have farms of servers in multiple locations to provide fail-safe uptime 7 days a week, 24 hours a day. Wikipedia identifies several types of services available via cloud computing:

- Infrastructure as a service (IaaS)
- Platform as a service (PaaS)
- Software as a service (SaaS)
- Storage as a service (STaaS)
- Security as a service (SECaaS)
- Data as a service (DaaS)
- Test environment as a service (TEaaS)
- Desktop as a service (DaaS)
- API as a service (APIaaS)

Since these services are provided to users anywhere, at any time, simply by connecting through the Internet, the physical location of their source is irrelevant. Hence, people refer to the location as being in "the Cloud".

How Office 2013 Uses Cloud-Computing

Office 2013 falls into the category, Software as a Service (SaaS). Office 2013 uses the cloud in several ways that will be explained in paragraphs within this section. For now, we can summarize how Office 2013 uses the cloud with an example. A user saves a document into some form of online storage. If the document is personal, the online storage might be a SkyDrive. If the document was created for business, the storage might be provided by an online SharePoint service (both SkyDrive and SharePoint will be explained later). The user can then access and edit the online document using any computing device. If the Office 2013 application is not installed on the user's device, it can be streamed to the user via an Internet connection using a new technology called, "Office on Demand". Personal settings are also stored in the cloud so the user experiences a similar look and feel regardless of the computing device. This is how Office 2013 uses cloud-computing.

Streaming from the Cloud

On July 16, 2012 when the Office 2013 preview was released to the public, Steve Ballmer, CEO of Microsoft, announced that Office 2013 was "designed from the get-go to be offered as a service." This caused a bit of confusion among those uninitiated to the Microsoft concept of this technology because Office 2013 runs completely from the desktop, which doesn't match some people's definition of "streaming."

The Office 2013 installer is based on the Microsoft App-V (application virtualization) technology. Traditionally, application virtualization requires applications to run on a remote machine, but not so with Office 2013. With Office 2013, the desired application runs within Windows and is connected through Click-to-Run (integratedoffice.exe). The application is then downloaded from the Microsoft Office 365 cloud service and locally cached onto the user's computing device. This is how Office 2013 can run alongside an existing Windows installation of a previous version of Office without conflict. Pretty cool, huh?

Microsoft introduced Click-to-Run in several prior versions of Office: it was a feature of the Professional Plus program of the Office 365 cloud service, and an option for Microsoft Office Home and Student 2010, and

Microsoft Office Home and Business 2010 (if purchased as a download rather than a retail-box), and the Microsoft Office Starter 2010 free trial.

The Click-to-Run installer is 400KB. When it's downloaded and launched by an Office user from an Office 365 site, it plays a brief video. The purpose of the video is mostly to buy time for the installer to pull down the Office components requested by the user. By the time the install passes the initial user configuration, most of the Office 2013 applications the user requested are functional; however, features can still continue to download in the background during the streaming process.

The Microsoft App-V also transfers the user's experience settings. These settings are stored in the user's online Office account. Dictionary files and other preferences, the user's SkyDrive or SharePoint file locations, are all stored up in the cloud. Whenever the user is authenticated to his/her Office account, the Microsoft application virtualization technology automatically streams the user's personal settings, including connections to cloud storage, and the user's "recent documents" menu.

Of course, one of the greatest benefits of streaming is the way it supports software updates. Office 2013 runs beautifully disconnected from the Internet; however, when it detects a connection has been re-established, Office 2013 checks the Microsoft cloud service for new components. If new components are available, the streaming technology will upgrade or patch Office 2013 in the background without user intervention.

Office on Demand

Office on Demand is a technology that can deliver an Office application (i.e., Word, Excel or PowerPoint) on demand to a user's PC. For example, the PC could be in a library, at a hotel business center, or it could even be a laptop the user borrowed from a friend. The few requirements are that the PC be connected to the Internet and running Windows 7 or later.

With Office on Demand, the application is "streamed" almost instantly to the user's PC without being permanently installed on it. Once the user logs off the PC, the application and documents that were temporarily streamed are no longer available to other users of that PC.

Microsoft has been cooking this recipe for several years. About the same time that Office 2010 was released, Microsoft Office users were provided access to Office Web Apps which have been web-based versions of Word, Excel, PowerPoint, and OneNote hosted by Microsoft in the cloud (or on a business customer's SharePoint Server). Office Web Apps are minimal, stripped-down, applications designed to compete with Google Docs. In contrast, Office on Demand downloads rich, full-featured, temporary installations of the Office applications. Office on Demand is initiated by logging into the user's account on the Office 2013 website. The application requested is then streamed to the user's local computer. When the user is finished with it, the application disappears!

Paul Barr, Lead Program Manager at Microsoft, summarized this experience in a post[1] on the Office team blog. His post stated, "What if you could use all the powerful features of the Office applications without doing an install at all?...Wouldn't that be the ultimate 'installation experience'?" Barr continued to write that Office on Demand applications must always be launched from the Office website; they do not install shortcuts or register file extensions on the host machine; and, the applications cannot be launched except through the browser.

Office on Demand is user-friendly. Customers do not need to enter a serial number or have administrative rights on their PCs to download and launch applications. The downloaded application is ready for use in as little time as a minute, in some cases only 15 seconds, depending on the user's internet connection. Office on Demand is made possible through the streaming capability of the Microsoft App-V application virtualization technology discussed in the previous section of this book.

According to Barr, installs using the new Click-to-Run technology have a higher success rate than Windows Installer based packages, and allows Office 2013 to run alongside a previous version of Office. For the first time, users can even run two different versions of Outlook at once! However, mixing 32-bit and 64-bit versions of Office is still not possible.

Barr also writes that another benefit of Office on Demand is that the Office website always delivers the latest version of apps, which eliminates the need for updates or patches immediately following an installation.

Office 2013 subscription customers can access Office on Demand versions of Word, Excel, PowerPoint, Access, Publisher, Visio, and Project. Users who opt to buy traditional desktop editions of Office 2013 may utilize SkyDrive as an online storage hub for documents; (Knowlton & Barr) however, they do not get the Office on Demand capability to stream Office 2013 apps. To get the Office on Demand benefit from the cloud, a user must purchase a subscription edition of Office 2013.

[1]Source: Click-to-Run and Office on Demand. Gray Knowlton and Paul Barr
http://blogs.office.com/b/office-next/archive/2012/08/27/click-to-run-and-office-on-demand.aspx

SkyDrive

"SkyDrive" is an online storage service hosted by Microsoft. The biggest benefit of SkyDrive is the fact that it is FREE! Anyone can sign-up for a free personal SkyDrive account at no cost.

What is SkyDrive?

A basic SkyDrive account is 7 GB of free storage. This is enough space for about 20,000 Office documents or 7,000 photos. This should be ample storage. If it isn't, you can add more storage for a small yearly fee.

SkyDrive Security

The files stored in SkyDrive are protected using the following security:

- Secure Sockets Layer (SSL) to encrypt your files when you upload or download them.

- Sophisticated physical and electronic security measures on the Microsoft servers to help keep your files safe.

- Redundant copies of each file saved on different servers and hard drives to help protect your data from hardware failure.

You can strengthen the security of your SkyDrive by creating a strong password and adding one or more proofs to your account. A "proof" is a phone number, email address, or trusted PC that can be used to recover your account if you ever lose access.

Access Any File, From Any Device

There are many cloud-based storage services available. Some of the more commonly known are Apple iCloud, Google Drive and Dropbox. None of them offer as much free storage as SkyDrive. None of them support all file types and computing devices as does SkyDrive. With SkyDrive, a user can securely store all types of files – documents, notes, photos, videos - then access these from any computing device. The computing device can be a PC, Mac, iPad, or any tablet or smartphone. Gone is the worry of forgetting files at home, school or work. The latest versions of saved files are always accessible on the user's SkyDrive.

Accessing files from SkyDrive is easy. It's a built-in function of Office 2013 located under File tab>Save As. It is the default save location for all of the subscription editions of Office 2013.

Phones and tablets can access files saved on SkyDrive by using a SkyDrive app. Apps are available for Windows Phone, iPhone, iPad, and Android devices. SkyDrive apps can be downloaded free of cost from the Microsoft SkyDrive website at http://windows.microsoft.com/skydrive

If the user has a device not supported by a specific app, SkyDrive can still be accessed by these devices. The user simply opens the phone or tablet web browser and goes to SkyDrive.com. The user signs in, finds the file or photo, and taps it.

Sharing Large Files

Ever run into size limits for email attachments? With SkyDrive you can email a link to a photo album or other large file so others can access it. Simply upload your file to your SkyDrive (up to 2GB from the SkyDrive app on your computer or 300MB from within SkyDrive.com), then select the files you want to send.

SkyDrive files can even be shared on Facebook, Gmail, Twitter, LinkedIn, or with any other contact or social network connected to your SkyDrive account. No doubt about it, SkyDrive is way cool, and it's an integral component to the new Office 2013.

Table 3. Comparing Cloud-based Storage Services

Free File Storage and Access	SkyDrive	Apple iCloud	Google Drive	Dropbox
Cloud storage	7 GB	5 GB*	5 GB	2 GB
Windows	●		●	●
Mac	●	●	●	●
Web	●		●	●
Remote access	●	●		
iPhone and iPad	●	*	●	●
Windows Phone	●			
Android	●		●	●
Mobile Web	●		●	●
Work Together Online				
Works with Microsoft Office for PC, Mac and web-devices	●			
Allows simultaneous editing	●		●	
Track versions	●		●	●
Free note-taking apps for your phone	●	*		
Showcase Photos				
Online slide shows	●	●	**	●
Email slide shows	●		**	
Post to Facebook & Twitter	●			●
Captions	●	●	**	●
Show geotags	●	●	**	●
Simple File Sharing				
Share with anyone	●		●	●
Online viewing for Office files	●		●	
Large file support (free)	2 GB		5 GB	2 GB
Options (annual price)				
Free storage	7 GB	5 GB	5 GB	2 GB
Add 20 GB	$ 10	$ 40		
Add 50 GB	$ 25	$100		
Add 100 GB	$ 50		$ 60	$ 99

*iCloud lets you store only specific types of files like photos for free. To store iWork documents in the cloud, you need to purchase iWork apps separately.

**Google Drive is for document storage. Google offers separate products—Google+ and Picasa—for photo storage and sharing.

Source: http://windows.microsoft.com/en-US/skydrive/compare

Demonstration - How to Create a SkyDrive Account

In this book, we will explore the new features of Office 2013 using fictitious files that you won't want populating your personal or business SkyDrive account. _Do not use your personal or business SkyDrive account to perform the demonstrations in this book!_ Instead, create a new account.

1. Go to **http://skydrive.com**

2. Complete the user profile (Use a different login if you already have a SkyDrive account).

3. **Sign-in**

4. Customize your SkyDrive account, if you'd like

5. To **logout**, click your name in the upper-right corner then from the drop-down menu select **Sign out**.

SharePoint Online

As an alternative to SkyDrive, subscribers to business editions of Office 2013 have the option to store their files in the cloud using SharePoint Online. SharePoint Online offers all of the storage benefits of SkyDrive along with expanded sharing capabilities for business organizations such as collaboration, search, metadata, workflow and compliance. For Office 2013 users, the primary advantage of SharePoint storage versus the consumer's SkyDrive storage is the management of co-authoring.

Co-Authoring

Co-authoring manages multiple users who are simultaneously working on the same document. This capability requires no additional server setup and is the default status for documents that are stored in SharePoint 2013 document libraries. Here are some recent changes to co-authoring which benefits users of Office 2013:

- Co-authoring is now supported in Word Web App and PowerPoint Web App.

- Other editors who join co-authoring a document can be seen faster in Word 2013, Excel 2013, and PowerPoint 2013.

- Updates are faster when multiple users co-author in the same OneNote page.

- Users can view, add, and reply to comments in Word Web App and PowerPoint Web App.

- Word files that contain revision marks can now be opened by users in in Word Web App.

- Users can easily set document permissions and send sharing notifications by using the Share with People feature in Office 2013 and SharePoint 2013.

Office Store

On August 6, 2012 Microsoft opened the "Office Store". The Office Store is a central depository of apps that expand the capabilities of Office 2013. One of the new features found on the Insert tab of the Ribbon within all the applications of Office 2013 is a button labeled "Apps for Office". Click this button and you'll be connected to the Office Store. Inventory in the store is organized by application (i.e. Word, Excel, Outlook) and include apps for purchase and free apps.

Apps expand the capabilities of Office 2013 by connecting to information sources on the web, or to applications outside of Office. Examples include dictionaries, legal forms, calendars, maps, and other useful tools. In the Office Store, users can read reviews before acquiring an app. All apps that are listed on the Office Store are validated so users can trust them. The apps are also based on web-standards, so they load easily.

All apps are cloud-aware! This means if you use a new machine, simply click on the "Apps for Office" button on your Ribbon, sign-in with your Microsoft account, and all your apps will appear. If you send a document to another user that was created using a specific app, a reference to the app travels with the document so the recipient can acquire the app, too!

Demonstration – Adding a Dictionary App

Adding an app from the Office Store is easy. Add a dictionary to Word 2013 by following these steps:

1. Launch Word 2013.

2. Select the **Insert** tab.

3. In the center of the tab, click **Apps for Office>See All...**

4. A pop up listing popular apps is displayed. If you don't see the **Merriam-Webster Dictionary**, type the word *Merriam* in the search box.

5. Click **Add** and follow the instructions.

6. After you've added an app (free or purchased) a record of your installation is stored in the cloud so you can access it and reinstall it from any device. Simply click on **Apps for Office>See All...** in the upper-left of the pop up, choose **MY APPS**. You must be logged into your Microsoft account (i.e., SkyDrive) to see your apps. Select the app you want to install/reinstall then click the **Insert** button.

7. To close the apps window, click the **Cancel** button or the in the upper-right corner.

General Changes in Office 2013

Microsoft had a few obvious goals when updating all of the applications in Office 2013.

- Integrate the suite with cloud services which allow users access to both content and apps from anywhere.

- Enhance the user experience by improving things users already do.

- Inherit the new Metro-style when running on the Windows 8 operating system, but still look familiar to users of previous Office versions.

- Include support for all user devices, such as keyboard/mouse equipped computers, and pen/touch capable tablets and phones.

- New features have been added to most applications, but the above goals influenced changes made to the foundation of Office 2013.

Cloud-based Resources and Storage

When you launch Office 2013, the first change you'll notice is Office 2013 prefers the cloud to store user preferences, documents, templates, add-in apps, and other resources. User preferences - such as dictionaries, the "recent documents" menu, connections, and personal settings - are stored in the cloud and streamed whenever the user is authenticated to his/her Office account. This is very beneficial to users who access their content from multiple computing devices. Templates are provided from Office.com as a cloud-based service that can be searched and accessed directly from within each of the Office 2013 applications.   The same is true for add-in apps that are available from the new online Office Store.

The default storage location for user documents created with consumer editions of Office 2013 is SkyDrive. For documents created with business editions of Office 2013, the default storage location is SharePoint Online. Either of these cloud-based online storage options allow a user to share documents with others and post links to documents on social media sites.

Co-editing Improvements

Collaboration is greatly enhanced in Office 2013 by embedding personal information about each reviewer who comments or marks up a shared document. Simply click the reviewer's embedded personal information to launch an Instant Message, Lync, or Skype call with that person!

Resume Reading

Another new feature found in all of the Office 2013 applications is "Resume Reading". When a user exits a document, Resume Reading stores a bookmark in the cloud so the user can return to the exact location on the document when it is reopened.   Resume Reading works even if the user opens the document from another device.

Touch, Stylus and Pen Support

Office 2013 integrates with the touch capabilities of the new Windows 8 operating system to provide quicker access to Office features when using a tablet or mobile device. If your PC has a touchscreen, Office 2013 automatically places a Touch Mode button on the quick address toolbar. Press the Touch Mode button and the interface changes with bigger buttons and more space to touch them so you don't accidently bump the wrong thing. This makes Office 2013 touch-friendly without making it inefficient to use a mouse and keyboard.

Improvements have also been made for pen and stylus support.   Of course, all of the Office 2013 applications inherit the new Metro-look user interface when run on the Windows 8 operating system.

Minor Look and Feel Changes

Other general changes to Office 2013 are minor, yet noticeable.   This includes a new color scheme that gives the applications a simpler look and flatter Ribbon compared to the 3D looking Ribbons of Office 2007 and Office 2010. The user also has the option to autohide the Ribbon to allow more document workspace.

What's New in Word 2013?

Word 2013 received some new features plus enhancements that improve performance. Several enhancements focus on supporting co-editing. There have also been improvements made to the user experience when reading documents on mobile devices, such as tablets and phones. The following is a brief summary. For details and hands-on demonstrations, read the chapter in this book titled, "New Features of Word 2013".

Read Mode

Remember the "Full Screen Reading" view introduced in Office 2007? It has been replaced in Office 2013 with a new "Read Mode" view. Today, more and more users are reading Word documents online rather than print. The new Read Mode view is a performance enhancement that reflows text automatically into columns to accommodate varying screen sizes. This makes it easier to read Word documents on the smaller screens of tablets and mobile devices.

Object Zoom

Users can now zoom tables, charts, images, or online videos by tapping a finger or clicking a mouse on the object. After viewing the object's detail, another finger tap or mouse click returns the object to its original size.

Co-editing

To further support collaboration online, Microsoft has added a co-editing capability to Office 2013 called, "Share". Share allows multiple people to collaboratively review or modify documents stored on the user's SkyDrive. When saving a document to SkyDrive, the author can choose who to share with, how to share (edit or just read), and whether to share with more people or to invite just one. The link to the document can then be emailed, or embedded on a blog or social network page.

Other features have been added to support collaboration. One is a new tracking option called, "Simple Markup" which provides an uncomplicated view of your document with red-line indicators to mark paragraphs and lines where tracked changes have been made.

Another new collaboration feature is a Reply button in the upper-right of each Comment balloon which allows reviewers to comment about other comments adjacent to the relevant text. After a comment no longer requires attention, it can be marked as done. It is then greyed out, but the conversation remains if you need to revisit it later.

You'll also notice that the reviewers are identified within comments by name and photo. Hover over the reviewer's photo and a Contact Card appears. You can click icons within the card to contact the reviewer using Instant Messenger, voice, video or email. You can even click a link to schedule a meeting using Outlook.

Finally, if you want to prevent other reviewers from accidently turning off tracking changes you can "Lock Tracking" with a password.

Presenting Online

What if you simply want to share your document with others as you read through it? You can now send people a link, and as you read through the document on your screen, they can follow along in their browsers. They don't even need Word to view the document!

Users of a business or professional edition of Word 2013 can take collaboration to a higher level. They can opt to collaborate with others via a Lync conversation or meeting. With Lync, the author can grant other participants in the meeting live control of the Word document. This has obvious benefits to business collaborators who are spread across geographic locations.

PDF Reflow

Perhaps one of the most exciting new features of Word 2013 is the ability to open a PDF document and edit its content. The new PDF reflow feature works so well that you get a Word document that looks like the original PDF - complete with fonts, layout, images, tables, charts and page numbers – except it's all editable! Opening the PDF is so fast that it takes only a few seconds longer than opening the document in Acrobat Reader. The conversion is remarkably accurate.

Online Media

Two new buttons appear on the Insert tab. Online Pictures has replaced the Clip Art button of Office 2007 and Office 2010. This upgraded feature allows a user to insert clip art from Office.com or any source on the Internet. Online Video is a new button that allows a user to embed video from any source on the Internet, such as YouTube.

Alignment Guides

Whenever you start to drag a chart, image, shape, video, or SmartArt towards the edge or center of a document, a guide will appear to mark the vertical center, the horizontal center, or margins on the page. The guides only appear when you need them and disappear when you're done.

Layout Options

Whenever you click on a chart, image, shape, video, or SmartArt, a button appears in the upper-right of the object that launches text wrapping options. These options are basically the same as Office 2007 and Office 2010; however, you can now access them from the selected object. Also, when you move, resize, or rotate an object, text reflows around it and appears as it would in its final position. Microsoft calls this "Live Layout".

Working with Tables

Three updates have been made to the table management features in Word 2013. You can now add a new row or column to a table by simply going to the location where the row is desired and clicking a button. Microsoft calls this new feature, "One-click Row/Column Insertion". Another new feature is a "Border Painter" that lets you apply borders by brushing them onto the table. Microsoft also refreshed the set of default table styles to provide more options for you to choose.

WordArt

The legacy WordArt tool from previous versions of Word has been replaced by the WordArt tool more similar to that found in Word 2010 and PowerPoint 2010. This allows you to do more than simply apply a WordArt style, but also to manipulate text effects, fills and outlines.

What's New in Excel 2013?

Some of the most noticeable enhancements made to Office 2013 are found in Excel. Collaboration capabilities have been enhanced slightly, but not as much as in Word or PowerPoint. The majority of improvements in Excel 2013 focus on making advanced formatting, charting and table features friendlier to mainstream users. The enhancements are summarized below. For details and hands-on demonstrations, read the chapter in this book titled, "New Features of Excel 2013".

Co-Editing

The same steps used to share documents and collaborate in Word 2013, apply to spreadsheets and workbooks in Excel 2013. When saving a workbook to SkyDrive or SharePoint, the author can choose who to share it with and the editing permissions. Just like in Excel 2010, the user can protect the workbook structure or restrict specific editing activity on a worksheet. After the Excel file is saved and sharing permissions setup, the user can send everyone involved an access link via email. Of course, the greatest advantage to collaborating within the cloud is that everyone is assured they are seeing the latest version. Excel also integrates with social networking by allowing you to embed a SkyDrive link on a blog or social network page that allows viewers to view or edit your spreadsheet.

Just like in Word 2013, users of a business or professional edition of Excel 2013 can also collaborate with others via Lync. With Lync, the owner can grant others in a conversation or meeting live control of a workbook so collaboration across distance is easier than ever before.

New Functions

Excel 2013 offers forty-eight new functions not available in previous versions. All are found in the Function Library group on the Formulas tab. Many have been added under the Math & Trig, Date & Time, Lookup & Reference, Logical, and Text buttons. Under the More Functions button, are new functions under the Statistical, Engineering, and Web categories. The new Web service category contains functions for referencing existing Representational State Transfer (REST)-compliant Web services. A list of all function additions and changes is provided in Chapter Four.

Flash Fill

A new button appears on the Data tab of Excel 2013. If you like Auto fill in earlier versions of Excel, you're going to love "Flash Fill". This new feature reads adjacent columns looking for similar formulas and formatting. The user simply begins filling data into a new column, then enables Flash Fill. If a pattern is recognized from adjacent columns, Excel automatically completes the remaining entries in the new column with no formulas or macros required! Flash Fill can extract data, concatenate, reverse last and first names, insert letters or symbols or numbers. This is one of the most amazing time-saving features of Excel 2013!

Quick Analysis Tool

When a user selects a range of data on a spreadsheet, Excel 2013 pops up a box in the lower-right of the selection containing "Quick Analysis" options. The options are a recommended set of analytic actions that offer a live preview of the data by applying one or more of the following:

- **Formatting** - Color Scales, Data Bars, Icon Sets, and more;
- **Charts** – Excel 2013 will recommend the most appropriate display;
- **Totals** – Sum, Average, Count, % of Total, and others;
- **Tables** – Simple tables and PivotTable variations;
- **Sparklines** – Line, Column, and Win/Loss

Of course, these data displays are not new to Excel and existed in previous versions. The Quick Analysis tool simply makes them more accessible to a user with a single click!

Recommended Charts

Speaking of recommended Charts, Excel 2013 is capable of recognizing patterns in your data and suggesting charts that best illustrate these patterns. This feature can be accessed through the Quick Analysis tool options, or from a button on the Insert tab called, "Recommended Charts". After selecting a data range, simply enable the button on the Ribbon and Excel 2013 will display a list of chart thumbnails populated with your data!

Chart Formatting Control

Formatting charts in Excel 2013 is quick and easy. When a chart is selected, three new option boxes appear to the right of the chart – Chart Elements, Styles/Colors, and Filters. Within each of these boxes are thumbnails that offer a Live Preview of your data if the option is applied. This makes it quick and easy to change the title, layout, color, style, or other elements of a chart.

Chart Animation

If you change a data entry in a chart's table, you will see the affect immediately with another new feature Microsoft calls, "Chart Animation". When you change the table data, Excel's chart engine animates that portion of the chart to show how the new value affects the visualization. Even the scale of the axes can change to match!

Recommended PivotTables

For many Excel users, one of the most valuable new features to Office 2013 is "Recommended PivotTables". This new feature is a button on the Insert tab and it is also one of the options in the Quick Analysis toolbox. Just like the Recommended Charts button, the gallery of suggested PivotTables is pre-populated with a live preview of the data you've selected so you can simply choose the PivotTable that looks the best.

The Excel Data Model used in Office 2013 provides analysis features that were previously only available by installing the PowerPivot add-in. This allows you to create PivotTables based on multiple tables in Excel. By importing different tables, and creating relationships between them, you can analyze data with results not available with traditional PivotTable data. When using multiple tables, you can now connect to and import data from additional data sources such as OData, Windows Azure DataMarket, and SharePoint data feeds. You can also connect to data sources from additional OLE DB providers.

The PivotTable and PivotCharts Options tab found in previous versions of Excel has been replaced with an "Analyze" tab in Excel 2013. A fun new feature added to the "Analyze" tab is Timeline Filters.

Timeline Filters

Would you like to compare your PivotTable or PivotChart data over different time periods? Instead of regrouping your data by dates, you can now filter data as it occurs over sequential time periods such as daily, monthly, quarterly, or yearly.

Power View

Many of the features that were in Power View for SharePoint 2010 are now integrated into Excel 2013. Power View is a reporting tool that provides interactive data exploration, visualization, and presentation. With a Power View report, you can pull your data together in tables, matrices, maps, and charts in an interactive view that can bring your data to life.

PowerPivot

The same PowerPivot add-in that enhanced the capabilities of Excel 2010 when combined with SharePoint 2010 is now natively integrated into Office Professional Plus 2013; you simply need to enable it. Once enabled, a new PowerPivot tab will appear on the Excel 2013 Ribbon.

PowerPivot is an advanced feature that allows you to build data models. Use it to define your own Calculated Fields, Key Performance Indicators (KPIs), filter imported data, and Detect Relationships.

Inquire Add-in

Another useful add-in included with Office Professional Plus 2013 is a new "Inquire" tool. This tool analyzes workbooks for data dependencies, formula errors, hidden information and broken links. The Inquire tool can diagram relationships between cells, worksheets and workbooks. It also contains a Compare Files feature to compare two versions of a workbook and a Clean Excess Cell Formatting button. All of these features are contained on a new Inquire tab that appears when the add-in is enabled.

What's New in PowerPoint 2013?

Only a few new features have been added to PowerPoint 2013. Instead, the focus is to help users get the most out of the features that existed in

PowerPoint 2007 and PowerPoint 2010. As with all the Office 2013 applications, PowerPoint 2013 has tighter cloud integration to better support collaboration with other users. The new features that have been added are enhancements to the presenter's mode, color-editing, charting, templates, and a capability to merge shapes. The following is a brief summary. For details and hands-on demonstrations, read the chapter titled, "New Features of PowerPoint 2013".

Theme Variants

Start PowerPoint 2013 and the first thing you'll notice are wider templates. The new default templates have a 16:9 aspect ratio to accommodate the wider screens of today's computers. After you choose a template, the next screen allows you to change the color-scheme.

Eyedropper

To precisely control color, the shape-fill and text-fill buttons under the Drawing Tools tab now include an "Eyedropper" option. The Eyedropper tool allows you to sample a color in a photo or elsewhere in your presentation to make the colors between text and images consistent.

Co-editing

The same steps used to share documents and collaborate in Word and Excel 2013 apply to PowerPoint 2013. When saving a presentation to SkyDrive or SharePoint, the author can choose who to share it with and the editing permissions. After the PowerPoint file is saved and sharing permissions setup, the user can send everyone involved an access link via email. Again, the greatest advantage to collaborating within the cloud is that everyone is assured they are seeing the latest version.

Another improvement to PowerPoint 2013 is to Comments. In earlier versions of PowerPoint, comments on slides resembled Post-it notes. PowerPoint 2013 offers the same enhancement as Word 2013 with a Reply button available in the upper-right of the Comment balloon. This "Reply to Comment" feature allows reviewers to comment on comments.

Just like in Word 2013, reviewers are identified within comments by name and photo. Hover over the reviewer's photo and a contact card appears.

You can click icons within the card to contact the reviewer using Instant Messenger, voice, video or email. You can even click a link to schedule a meeting using Outlook.

Also, just like in Word and Excel 2013, users of a business or professional edition of PowerPoint 2013 can take collaboration to a higher level with Lync. A PowerPoint author can opt to collaborate with others via a Lync conversation or meeting. With Lync, the author can grant other participants in the meeting live control of a PowerPoint presentation.

Inserting Online Images, Video and Audio

On a computing device connected to the Internet, PowerPoint 2013 can access images from Office.com, Bing, and other services. This improvement allows you to directly add images to a presentation from the Web without having to save them first to your desktop.

PowerPoint 2013 now supports .mp4, .m4v, and .mov video formats in addition to the .asf, .avi, .mpg (.mpeg), .swf and .wmv formats supported in PowerPoint 2010. Likewise, .m4a and .mp4 audio formats are now supported in PowerPoint 2013 in addition to the legacy .aiff, .au, .mid (.midi), .mp3, .wav and .wma audio formats supported in earlier versions. So, you no longer need to convert .mp4 video and audio formats before using them in your PowerPoint 2013 presentation. In fact, for the best playback experience Microsoft recommends using .mp4 videos encoded with H.264 video (a.k.a. MPEG-4 AVC) and AAC audio.

Alignment Guides

Guides existed in previous versions of PowerPoint; however, they now have enhanced capabilities. Guides can now be placed in a unique location on each Slide Master Layout, so they are displayed in that exact same location on every slide that uses the layout.

When you enable the legacy guides, another set of guides are also enabled in PowerPoint 2013 called, "Alignment Guides". These new Alignment Guides operate the same as in Word 2013. Simply drag a chart, image, shape, video, or SmartArt towards the edge or center of the slide, and an Alignment Guide automatically appears to mark the vertical center, or margins on the slide. These special Alignment Guides appear only when you need them and disappear when you're done. Alignment Guides are most useful when you want to quickly center objects, or align them with the text margin of a slide.

Merge Shapes

On the Format tab of the Drawing Tools, in the Shapes group, is a new "Merge Shapes" button. The options under this new button are Union, Combine, Fragment, Intersect, and Subtract. These new tools allow you to merge two or more shapes into a new shape. This is much more convenient than building shapes in Visio and copying them to PowerPoint.

Presenter View

"Presenter View" in PowerPoint 2013 has new features to help you better engage your audience and stay organized. The new features include:

- **Auto-extend** - When projecting to a screen, this setting ensures the speaker notes and navigation tools are displayed on the monitor only you can see.

- **Navigation Grid** - This new feature allows you to jump around in a presentation without the audience's awareness. You can show slides in and out of sequence. The Navigation Grid is especially useful when answering questions at the end of a presentation.

- **Slide Zoom** – In PowerPoint 2013, you can direct your audience's attention by zooming in on a chart, or graphic with a couple of clicks. This is a very useful tool for displaying details during discussions.

What's New in OneNote 2013?

If you're not a user of Microsoft OneNote, you're missing out. It is a digital notebook for gathering notes, links, webpages, sketches, and media, into a single collection. OneNote links to all of the other Office applications and is now included in all editions of Office 2013, except Mac. OneNote 2013 is not much different than OneNote 2010, except that it has been optimized to run on either Windows 7 or Windows 8. If run on Windows 8, OneNote inherits the Metro look and touch capabilities allowing you to draw, type, click or swipe. Aside from that, a new bookmarking feature has been added to support the "Resume Reading" enhancement integrated into all Office 2013 applications, and OneNote now allows Excel and Visio components to be embedded onto a note page. Syncing with SkyDrive and SharePoint is also faster. That's about all that's changed in OneNote 2013. The following is a summary. For details and hands-on demonstrations, read the chapter titled, "New Features of OneNote 2013".

Improved Search

In OneNote 2013, searching is faster and more versatile. You can search for terms in a note, title of a file, or even text in the caption of a picture. Basically, you can search for any term you've captured.

Co-editing

Although you can choose to save your notes to any location, they are saved online to SkyDrive or SharePoint by default. This makes sharing easy. Simply send your friends a link to the file and grant them the necessary permissions to view or edit. Since the notes are stored online, you can be assured that everyone is accessing the latest version. Storing online assures that your notes are always up to date on all your devices.

As in previous versions, OneNote automatically saves your notes so you can't forget. You can also export notebooks, sections, or pages.

Support for Mobile and Touch Devices

OneNote has Mobile apps for Windows Phone, iOS devices, and Android phones. If a mobile app doesn't yet exist for your particular device, simply use an Internet browser with the OneNote Web App!

On touch capable devices, you can change from Mouse Mode to Touch Mode to add more space between buttons so it is easier to control OneNote with your finger.

Converting Handwritten Notes to Type

OneNote 2013 allows you to draw and edit with a finger or stylus. If you'd rather write than type, handwriting conversion in OneNote 2013 can convert your writing to text more accurately than previous versions.

Embedded Files

One of the most powerful uses of OneNote is its capability to insert pictures, documents, videos, and more into your notes. In OneNote 2013, if you insert an Excel spreadsheet, you also get a preview of possible charts and diagrams that will appear next to your notes. If you update the Excel file, your preview updates automatically.

Enhanced Tables

Table tools have been enhanced in OneNote 2013 to support making headers and to rearrange rows and columns. With a single click, you can also convert a table in your notes into an embedded Excel spreadsheet.

Send to OneNote Utility

This new feature lets you clip items, web pages and documents, or create quick notes to send to OneNote 2013 even when the application is closed.

What's New in Outlook 2013?

Outlook is included in all editions of Office 2013 except the traditional edition, Office Home and Student. Significant performance improvements have been made to Outlook 2013. It is now possible to synchronize Contacts, Mail and Calendars with popular email services, such as Hotmail. Social networking with Facebook and LinkedIn are now fully integrated into Outlook 2013. Other improvements include better searching, a weather bar addition to calendars, mail tips, and a pop-up window within the email reading pane that displays relevant information about contacts, appointments and tasks. The following is a brief summary of these enhancements. For details and hands-on demonstrations, read the chapter, "New Features of Outlook 2013".

Exchange ActiveSync Support

Previous versions of Outlook provided synchronization of email but nothing else. Many frustrated users discovered Calendars and Contacts could not be synchronized natively with Outlook. The new Exchange ActiveSync feature corrects that shortfall. Exchange ActiveSync makes it possible for Outlook 2013 to synchronize calendar appointments, contacts and email from many popular email services. This provides Hotmail and other email services enhanced push capabilities to Outlook 2013.

Navigation Bar

The Navigation Pane which resided on the left side of Outlook 2007 and Outlook 2010 has been simplified to a Folder Pane supporting just email. Mail, Calendar, People, Tasks and Navigation Options are now located on a "Navigation Bar" across the bottom of the Outlook window.

Peeks

Another new feature of Outlook 2013 is something Microsoft is calling, "Peeks". Simply hover over Calendar, People, or Tasks on the Navigation Bar and get a pop-up view of your favorite contacts, monthly calendar, or active tasks. No longer do you need to leave what you're doing to access this information, instead you can simply peek at it!

Social Network Connectors

Click the "Account Settings" button under the File tab and you'll see an option to add and configure Social Networking Accounts. Built-in integration exists for Facebook, LinkedIn, and Windows Live Messenger. Microsoft will add support for other providers as they become available.

People Card

Adding email accounts and social networking accounts to Outlook can create duplicate contact cards. Outlook 2013 merges contact cards for the same person into a single view called a "People Card".

Mail Enhancements

A couple of very useful features have been added to email.

- **In-line Replies** – allows you to quickly Reply, Reply All or Forward from within the reading pane instead of opening an editing pane.

- **MailTips** – is a dialog box that warns you about common mistakes, such as your email recipient is out of the office, or you forgot to attach a document, and other useful warnings.

Meeting Enhancements

A few new features have been added to the business editions and the Office Professional Plus 2013 edition of Outlook.

- **Lync Meeting** – sets up a Lync Meeting as easily as scheduling a regular meeting. The meeting link and call-in phone numbers are automatically added to the meeting request.

- **Meeting Notes** – allows you to add notes to the meeting using OneNote or open notes already associated with the meeting.

- **Time Zones** – adds a time zone field to the meeting Start/End time.

- **Room Finder** – opens a list of available rooms (configured on the Exchange Server), a monthly calendar, and a list of suggested times.

Weather Bar

A "Weather Bar" has been added to Calendars in Outlook 2013. This feature provides a simple three-day forecast for any location you configure. The temperature can be displayed in either Fahrenheit or Celsius. The Weather Bar can be useful when planning special appointments, such as meetings on the golf course!

Improved Search

In Outlook 2013, you can search information more quickly in email, attachments, calendar appointments, and contacts.

What's New in Access 2013?

Enhancements to Access 2013 focus less on it being a database and more on it being a database app development tool. Access is included in all editions of Office 2013 except the traditional editions of Office Home and Student, and Office Home and Business. Access 2013 installs only on a PC. It is now easier to build apps that run on the web with little knowledge of software development. The following is a brief summary of these enhancements. For details and hands-on demonstrations, read the chapter, "New Features of Access 2013".

App Templates

Included in Access 2013 are professionally designed app templates to help you run your business with little knowledge of software development.

Table Templates

Access 2013 uses table templates to create apps to track your data. Simply type your data and Access handles the complexities of fields, relationships, and rules by creating a tracking table. This allows you to focus on the data of your project while Access creates the user interface.

Drill and Peek

In Access 2013, you can "Drill" into data details represented by a hyperlink in a field, and then "Peek" at relevant information that appears in a pop-up.

Autocomplete

Drop-down menus and recommendations appear when you type data to help you make accurate entries.

Data Storage and Control

Access apps are stored in Microsoft SQL Azure/Server which provides security, scalability, disaster recovery, back-up and restore, for your data. Access apps are made available to users through a connection to SharePoint, or from an on-premises server via a browser. The advantage of accessing through SharePoint is that Access apps can leverage SharePoint user access control and centralized management features.

What's New in Publisher 2013?

Publisher is included in all editions of Office 2013 except the traditional editions of Office Home and Student, and Office Home and Business. Publisher 2013 has more templates, improved styles and text effects, a scratch area for importing pictures, new tools for editing images, and better support for exporting projects for commercial printing. The following is a brief summary of these enhancements. For details and hands-on demonstrations, read the chapter, "New Features of Publisher 2013".

Templates

Microsoft has dedicated more resources than ever on templates in Publisher 2013. You'll now find a variety of templates to help you create labels, flyers, invitations, calendars, business cards, certificates, signs, brochures, newsletters, and other common documents.

WordArt

The new version of "WordArt" added to Word 2013 is now in Publisher 2013. It is not the legacy WordArt tool you may be familiar with from previous versions of Word, but it is more similar to the WordArt tool found in PowerPoint. This newer version of the tool allows you to do more than simply apply a WordArt style to text, but also to manipulate text effects, fills and outlines.

Scratch Area

Replacing and switching images is easier than in previous versions of Publisher. Previous versions required images to be inserted one at a time using either the "Picture" or "ClipArt" button. In Publisher 2013, you can select multiple images using either the "Pictures" or "Online Pictures" button. Rather than stacking all of your images onto the center of your page, like in previous versions of Publisher, the images are now placed in a workspace called a "Scratch Area" located to the right of your document. The Scratch Area displays thumbnails of your images until you use them in your document.

You can also drag an image from the scratch area until it's over an existing image and a pink highlight appears around the existing image. Release your mouse and the two images switch places.

Live Picture Swap

Hover over any image in a Publisher 2013 document and an icon will appear in the center of the image that controls, "Live Picture Swap". When two images are selected, clicking this icon will swap the images. Formatting is unaltered, such as size, borders or effects.

Picture Backgrounds

Publisher 2013 provides more options when saving a picture as a background. When using the "Background" button on the Page Design tab, you can now set its transparency, tile the image, and control aspects of tiling. A new feature is to simply right-click on an image and select "Save as Background" to apply it as either a Fill or Tile to your document.

Save for Photo Printing

In the "Pack and Go" section of Export under the File tab is a new feature called, "Save for Photo Printing". This feature saves each page of your document as either a JPEG or TIFF image which is ideal if you want to package your publication as a set of images to print at a photo center.

What's New in InfoPath 2013?

Unless you develop a lot of forms, you may not be familiar with Microsoft InfoPath: InfoPath Designer is used to build forms; InfoPath Filler is used to complete non-web forms. InfoPath is commonly used with Microsoft SharePoint InfoPath Form Services. Because of its tight relationship with SharePoint, InfoPath 2013 is included only in Office 365 Small Business Premium and Office Professional Plus 2013.

Visual Studio Tools

Only cosmetic changes have been made to InfoPath 2013 compared to InfoPath 2010. The look has been updated to match the rest of Office 2013, but no new features have been added. The only noticeable change is the removal of Microsoft Visual Studio Tools for Applications IDE from Microsoft InfoPath Designer 2013. Now, if you want to write or edit form code, you must have Visual Studio 2012 and the Visual Studio Tools for Applications 11 add-on. The programming experience itself has not changed but a software developer can now use the full Visual Studio development experience when writing code for InfoPath forms. Because nothing has changed that affects the mainstream user of InfoPath 2013, there is no subsequent chapter in this book containing hands-on demonstrations of new features.

What's New in Lync 2013?

On January 25, 2011 Microsoft Office Communicator 2007 was replaced by Lync 2010. So, what is Lync? It is a communication platform that provides instant messaging, telephone conferencing, video support, desktop application and PowerPoint sharing, primarily to businesses.

To access all of these communication services requires each user to have a Lync client connected to a Lync server. Most mainstream Office users do not require these services, so the Lync 2013 client is included only in Office 365 Small Business Premium and Office Professional Plus 2013.

Enhanced Video Support

The Lync 2013 client can simultaneously display five different participants' videos. It identifies the active speaker during a meeting and participants are represented by HD photos. Lync 2013 uses open standards, including H.264 SVC, which enables HD video conferencing across a range of computing devices: desktop computers, laptops, tablets and phones.

Presenter Controls

If you are the presenter at a meeting, you'll notice the controls are designed to be accessible but not distracting. The controls automatically optimize for the audience size and the content available to the participants.

Improved Integration with Office 2013

Lync meetings can be launched from Outlook 2013. Within Outlook 2013 there is also a button to initiate note taking. Lync automatically captures participant lists into OneNote and participants can co-edit meeting notes directly from Lync, so they don't have to switch between applications. Any Office 2013 application can be shared across a Lync meeting.

Other Lync Enhancements

Other enhancements made to Lync are implemented on the server-side and not part of Office 2013. These enhancements will not be detailed in this book, but they are so exciting they deserve a mention. Here they are:

- **Lync-to-Skype Federation** – Lync 2013 can now connect to Skype users. This allows businesses to communicate with potential customers and businesses partners who have Skype, but do not have Lync.

- **Lync Mobile** – allows a user to send an IM, make a Lync call, or join a Lync Meeting from a Windows Phone, iOS or Android device.

- **Lync Web App** – both PC and Mac users can use a browser to join a Lync Meeting. The Lync Web App supports multiparty HD video, instant messaging, VoIP, and sharing of desktop applications.

Only the Lync 2013 client is included in Office 2013. The functionality of Lync is provided by a Lync server, not Office. So, there is no subsequent chapter in this book containing demonstrations of Lync features.

Chapter Summary

This chapter provided an overview of the changes in Office 2013 compared to earlier versions of Office.

Look and feel changes were discussed. When running on Windows 7, only slight cosmetic changes are noticed in the overall look of the user interface. When run on Windows 8, Office 2013 inherits the Metro-style look even though it runs in the Desktop side of Windows 8. You also learned that Office 2013 has been enriched with touch and pen capabilities making it easier to use on tablet and mobile devices.

The biggest change to Office 2013 is its shift into the cloud. Documents and settings can be stored in the cloud and the applications streamed to Windows 7 and Windows 8 desktops using Microsoft Click-to-Run technology. Click-to-Run makes Office on Demand possible because applications can now be streamed instantly to any PC without being permanently installed on it.

The online storage service hosted by Microsoft called, SkyDrive, was examined. Anyone can register for a free online account with 7 GB of storage and Microsoft will provide additional storage for a small annual fee. SkyDrive was compared to Apple iCloud, Google Drive, and Dropbox. Step-by-step instructions were given to setup a SkyDrive account.

SharePoint was mentioned as another online storage solution available to business users. The primary advantage of SharePoint over SkyDrive is its ability to manage co-authoring amongst multiple users.

The new Office Store was introduced which supplies apps for free and for purchase. Apps expand the capabilities of Office 2013 by connecting to information sources or applications outside of Office. Examples include dictionaries, legal forms, calendars, maps, and other useful tools.

The remainder of the chapter summarized the new features found in each of the Office 2013 applications. You learned that general changes made across the entire Office 2013 suite include a preference for cloud-storage of documents, templates, settings and add-in apps; better collaboration features; Resume Reading; touch and stylus support for tablets and phones; and changes to the look with a flatter Ribbon and simplified color scheme of White, Light Gray or Dark Gray.

The new features specific to Word 2013 are Read Mode, Object Zoom, improved Co-Editing, Presenting Online, PDF Reflow, support for inserting Online Pictures and Online Video, Alignment Guides, Layout Options, improved Table management, and improved WordArt.

Excel 2013 received new features to make advanced formatting, charting and tables more accessible to mainstream users. The new features include better Co-editing, more Functions, Flash Fill, a Quick Analysis Tool, Recommended Charts, Chart Formatting Control, Chart Animation, Recommended PivotTables, Timeline Filters, Power View, PowerPivot, and an Inquire add-in.

PowerPoint 2013 received only a few changes. Templates now have a 16:9 aspect ratio and allow the user to change color schemes. Other additions are an Eyedropper tool, improved Co-Editing features similar to Word 2013, Online Pictures, support for .mp4 video and audio formats, new Alignment Guides, Merge Shapes, and enhancements to Presenter View.

OneNote 2013 has improved Searching, enhancements for Co-editing, universal support for mobile and touch devices, and better conversion of handwritten notes into type. Excel and Visio components can now be embedded onto a note page and modified directly using their parent applications. Table formatting has been improved. A new utility called Send to OneNote can add items to OneNote even when the application is closed.

Outlook 2013 received significant performance improvements. It is now possible to synchronize Contacts, Mail and Calendars with popular email services, such as Hotmail. Social networking with Facebook and LinkedIn are now fully integrated into Outlook 2013. Other improvements include Searching and Sharing Calendars, a Weather Bar, and a feature called Peeks that display relevant information about contacts, appointments and tasks from within the Mail pane. There are also several enhancements to Meetings such as buttons to launch a Lync Meeting or access Meeting Notes, add Time Zones to meeting Start/End times, and a Room Finder.

Mail now allows In-line Replies and provides MailTips to warn if you forgot to attach a document or if your message is too long for your recipient.

New features added to Access 2013 include App Templates to aid in the development of database apps, Table Templates, Peek and Drill, and Autocomplete. Apps created with Access 2013 are designed to be stored in Microsoft SQL Azure/Server with user access control provided by SharePoint.

Publisher 2013 received several new features and enhancements. There are more Templates for starting publication projects, WordArt, a Scratch Area for managing images, Live Picture Swap, and better options for saving Picture Backgrounds. Another nice addition is a Save for Photo Printing feature that saves each page of your Publisher document as either a JPEG or TIFF image so you can print it at a photo center.

InfoPath 2013 received no new features, only a cosmetic change to match the other Office 2013 applications. The only significant change is the removal of Microsoft Visual Studio Tools for Applications IDE from Microsoft InfoPath Designer 2013. If you want to write or edit form code, you must now have Visual Studio 2012 and the Visual Studio Tools for Applications 11 add-on.

InfoPath 2013 and the Lync 2013 client are included only in the Office 365 Small Business Premium and Office Professional Plus 2013 editions. The new Lync 2013 client has enhanced video support and can now display up to five video channels using the H.264 SVC standard. Improvements have also been made to the Presenter controls. Lync 2013 is also more tightly integrated with Office 2013 so that a Lync Meeting can be launched from a button within Outlook 2013 and a list of Lync meeting participants is automatically captured by OneNote. All Office 2013 applications can be shared in a Lync meeting.

The remainder of this book is divided into chapters to help you master the new features added to each of the Office 2013 applications.

Chapter 3:
New Features of
Word 2013

This chapter covers the following topics:

- ✓ Read Mode
- ✓ Object Zoom
- ✓ Co-editing
- ✓ Presenting Online
- ✓ PDF Reflow
- ✓ Online Media
- ✓ Layout Options
- ✓ Alignment Guides
- ✓ Working with Tables
- ✓ WordArt

Our world is becoming more mobile and expects to read and edit documents on a variety of devices - such as tablets and phones - not just on computers, laptops, and netbooks.   People share millions of documents every day. They want to collaborate on their documents faster and in more intuitive ways. With these needs in mind, Microsoft has added several enhancements to Word 2013.

In this chapter, we will examine new features designed to make collaboration easier, such as Read Mode, Object Zoom, and several augmentations to Co-editing. We will explore Presenting Online which was introduced in PowerPoint 2010 and is now in Word 2013. We will also look at the new PDF Reflow which enables Word 2013 to edit PDF documents. Last of all, we will explore improvements to several familiar tasks making them faster and easier to perform. Mostly, these tasks involve working with images and tables. The features supporting these improvements are inserting Online Pictures and Online Video, Alignment Guides, Layout Options, a few enhancements to Tables, and a new version of WordArt.

To master the new features presented in this chapter, you are encouraged to follow along with the hands-on demonstrations. You may use or create your own files; however, specific files are referenced in the instructions to help you master these features more quickly. Refer to Chapter One in this book for instructions on how to download the demonstration files.

Read Mode

Have you ever wished that a Word document could behave more like a digital magazine? Welcome to **Read Mode**!

When you open a document in **Read Mode**, the Word Ribbon disappears and it's replaced by three tabs located in upper-left of the view screen: **File**, **Tools**, and **View**.

Navigating through the document is like turning pages in a magazine. To pan left or right, simply use the arrow keys on your keyboard or click your mouse. On touch-sensitive devices, like tablets and phones, you can flick your finger across the page.

Read Mode is designed to reflow the text to fit the size of your screen, whether it's a large monitor, tablet, or phone. Pictures, charts, or tables are also resized to fit the columns. You can control the number of columns, the contrast of the background to make the document more readable, and the size of the text.

Let's examine **Read Mode** and play with these features.

Demonstration – Exploring Read Mode

1. In Word 2013, select **File>Open**. Select the location where you unzipped the demonstration files you downloaded in Chapter One (i.e., SkyDrive or Computer). **Browse** *to Tours.docx.* Select it and click the **Open** button.

2. If your Word Ribbon is set to **Auto-hide**, you can display it by clicking the three dots in the upper-right corner of the window. You can reconfigure the Ribbon display by clicking the **Ribbon Display Options** icon, which is next to the **?** help icon. For the purpose of these demonstrations, reconfigure your Ribbon to **Show Tabs and Commands**. This will make the display of the Ribbon persistent.

3. On the Ribbon, select the **View** tab. In the **Views** group, select **Read Mode**. Depending on your screen size, the document will be displayed in one or more columns.

4. You are now ready to explore **Read Mode**. In the upper left corner are three tabs: **File**, **Tools** and **View**. The following paragraphs describe the options found under each of these tabs. Read the descriptions in the paragraphs and play with the options. Have fun!

5. When finished, return back to **Page Layout** view by selecting **View>Edit Document**.

File Tab

The **File** tab takes you to the normal **Backstage** view of the Ribbon.

Tools Tab

Four options are provided under the **Tools** tab. They are as follows:

- **Find** – allows you to search for a term in the document. Type the term, *bike*, to view all instances of the word *bike* highlighted in the document.

- **Search with Bing** – initiates a web search for the term entered, *bike*.

- **Undo** – removes previous edits, such as to a Comment.

- **Redo** – reverses **Undo**.

View Tab

Six options are provided under the **View** tab. They are as follows:

- **Edit Document** – returns the view back to **Print Layout**.

- **Navigation Pane** – provides three ways to navigate the document: **Headings**, **Pages**, and **Results**. Select each one to see the result.

- **Show Comments** – do you see the two comment icons on the first and last pages of the document? Select **Show Comments** to view their contents. To disable, click **Show Comments** again.

- **Column Width** – provides three widths: **Narrow**, **Default**, and **Wide**. Select each one to see the result. Whichever you choose, or if you rotate your tablet between landscape and portrait modes, the screen will be divided into equally sized columns that stay as close as possible to the column width you selected.

- **Page Color** – changes the document's contrast to accommodate different reading conditions. The default text color is black, but you can change the background of the document to **None** (White), **Sepia**, or **Inverse** (Black).

- **Layout** – directs the text flow into multiple columns or a single column with **Column Layout** and **Paper Layout**.

Zoom Slider

In the lower right-corner of the screen is a **Zoom** slider. Use the slider to scale the text to a size that is most comfortable for you.

Reference Options

Read Mode also has a mini-menu with several useful tools. Select a term in the document and **right-click** to pop-up the menu.

- **Copy** – copies the selected text onto the Windows clipboard. To demonstrate, select one of the terms *bike* **right-click** and select **Copy**. To verify that *bike* is on the Windows clipboard, open the Windows application **Notepad** and **Paste** the term into it.

- **Define** – opens a dictionary and retrieves a definition. In the first paragraph, last sentence, select *tent*. **Right-click** and select **Define**. A pop-up will display the definition. Depending on the dictionary app installed, other options may be displayed, such as synonyms or an audio button to hear the pronunciation of the word.

  Note: The first time you launch **Define**, the Office Store will provide a list of dictionary apps. Choose the **Merriam-Webster Dictionary** and install it.

- **Translate** – translates a term to another language. Select *tent*. **Right-click** and select **Translate**. A pane will open on the right. Using the dropdown menus, change the fields to be **From English** and **To Spanish**. A result will show in the lower pane.

- **Search with Bing** – initiates a web search for the term selected, *tent*.

- **New Comment** – adds a comment. Select a term in the document, then **right-click** and select **New Comment**. Reverse this action from the tab **Tools>Undo Insert Comment**.

- **Highlight** – marks selections. Select a paragraph, **right-click** and choose **Highlight**, and select a color. To reverse this action, from the menu at the top of the screen, click **Tools>Undo Highlight**.

Object Zoom

When a document is viewed in **Read Mode**, the text is reflowed and any pictures, charts, or tables are resized to fit the columns. Often these items are reduced from their original size which can sometimes make them difficult to read. You can zoom one of these objects with a double-click to enlarge it to its original size. After viewing the object's detail, another finger tap or mouse click returns the object to its original size.

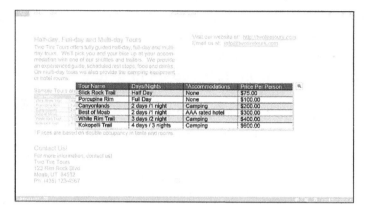

Demonstration – Object Zoom

1. If you just completed the **Demonstration – Read Mode**, skip this step. Otherwise, in Word 2013 select **File>Open**. Select the location where you unzipped the demonstration files you downloaded in Chapter One (i.e., SkyDrive or Computer). **Browse** to *Tours.docx*. Select it and click the **Open** button.

2. Locate the table on the last page of the document and **double-click** it. The table will enlarge to its normal size and be displayed in the center of the screen.

3. When finished viewing its details, simply **click once** anywhere outside the zoomed table to return to Read Mode.

4. If you'd like, you can repeat these steps to zoom a photo.

Co-editing

When saving a Word 2013 file to SkyDrive or SharePoint, the owner can choose who to share with and whether each invitee can view or edit the document. After the editing permissions are setup, the owner can send the invitees an access link via email. Of course, the greatest advantage of collaborating within the cloud is that your invitees are assured they are seeing the latest version of your document. Word 2013 also integrates with social networking sites by allowing you to embed a SkyDrive link on a blog or social network page that lets others view or edit your document.

Users of a business or professional edition of Word 2013 can also collaborate with others via Lync. With Lync, the owner can grant others in a conversation or meeting live control of the document so collaboration across distance is easier than ever before.

This section examines the enhancements that support co-editing in Word 2013: **Share**, **Simple Markup**, **Lock Tracking,** and **Reply to Comment**.

Share

Sharing documents on SkyDrive was introduced in Office 2010, but in Office 2013 it's simpler. Under the **File** tab in the **Backstage** view of Word 2013 is a new feature called, **Share**. This feature replaces Save & Send which was in Office 2010. All of the options that were in Save & Send still exist in **Share**, and few new ones have been added.

Demonstration – Sharing a Document on SkyDrive

1. If you just completed a previous demonstration in this chapter, skip this step. Otherwise, in Word 2013 select **File>Open**. Select the location where you unzipped the demonstration files that you downloaded in Chapter One (i.e., SkyDrive or Computer). **Browse** to *Tours.docx*. Select it and click the **Open** button.

2. Select **File>Share**. Four options will display: **Invite People, Email, Present Online,** and **Post to Blog**. Email and Post to Blog are the same as Word 2010 under Save & Send. Select **Invite People**.

3. When **Invite People** is selected, a button displays in the right pane called, **Save to Cloud**. Click it. This will actually take you to **File>Save As**. Three options are displayed under **Save As** which are: **SkyDrive**, **Computer** (i.e., local drive or network drive) and **Add a Place** (i.e., Office 365 SharePoint).

Note: A fourth option will display if you are signed into an Office 365 account, **Other Web Locations** (i.e., SharePoint or another online storage service).

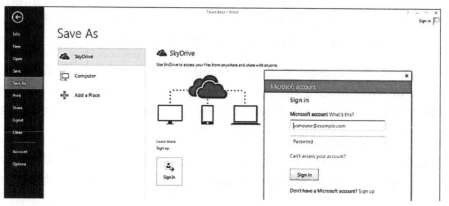

4. Select **SkyDrive**. A **Sign In** button will appear in the right pane.

5. Click **Sign In** and provide the credentials you created in Chapter Two. This connects Office 2013 to your SkyDrive. If you did not create a SkyDrive account in Chapter Two, click the Sign up link instead and create an account first, then **Sign In**.

6. When Word 2013 is connected to your SkyDrive, its name will be displayed and you will be provided a button to **Browse** it.

Note: If you later want to disconnect Word 2013 from an online service, such as SkyDrive, go to the **File>Account** option. Below your photo, click **Sign Out**. Or, for other connections, choose the **Connected Service** from the list and click the **Remove** link. To reconnect to SkyDrive, repeat steps 3 thru 6 above.

7. Click the **Browse** button. This will open your SkyDrive.

8. Create a **New Folder** named *Office 2013 Book Demos*. Save your *Tours.docx* document into this folder.

9. After you save your document to SkyDrive, Word 2013 will automatically return you to **Invite People**. In the top field, enter the email addresses of people with whom you want to share your document. You can validate the email addresses by clicking the first icon to the right of the name field. You can choose names from your Outlook Address Book by clicking the second icon to the right of the name field.

10. The drop-down menu to the right of the name field allows you to choose the access you are granting this specific list of people: **Can view** or **Can edit**.

11. You can also include a message in your invitation by typing it into the message field.

12. When you have finished configuring your invitation, click the **Share** button. SkyDrive may prompt you for additional information. If so, click the link for additional authentication and follow the instructions. An email will automatically be sent to your invitees that includes your message and link to your document. Your list of invitees displays under **Shared With** so you'll always know who can access this file.

Get a Sharing Link and Post to Social Networks

Permission to view or edit files on SkyDrive is embedded in the access link provided to a viewer. Once a file has been placed onto SkyDrive, you share it by sending others either a link to view, or a link to edit.

If you want your invitees to be identified on the document's **Share** pane, use **Invite People** to generate the access links. If listing each individual's identity on the **Share** pane is not important and you'd rather have the convenience of inviting people by group, you can **Get a Sharing Link** and send it in a bulk email. Another way to share with groups of people is to embed a link onto a web page, blog, or post it on a social networking site.

Demonstration – Generating a Sharing Link

1. This demonstration requires that you complete the previous **Demonstration – Sharing a Document on SkyDrive**. When you are connected to a workbook on SkyDrive, two new options will appear in Word 2013 under **File>Share**: **Get a Sharing Link** (or **Get a Link**) and **Post to Social Networks**. Select **Get a Sharing Link** (or **Get a Link**).

2. In the right pane are two fields: **View Link** and **Edit Link**. To the right of each of these empty fields is a button, **Create Link**. Click each of these buttons to generate the two types of links.

3. After generating the type of link you want, simply copy the link and paste it into a group email or onto a web page. Anyone who clicks the link will be taken to your document and have the level of access specified by the link. At the bottom of the pane, under **Shared With,** the links are listed to remind you of their existence for this file.

4. To test your links, copy the **View Link** you generated and paste it into your browser. This opens the workbook on SkyDrive. Notice that you can **Download** and **Find** items within the document, but you cannot **Share** it, nor edit anything. You have View access only.

5. Next, copy the **Edit Link** and paste it into your browser. Just like with View permission, you can **Download** and **Find** items in the document, but you cannot **Share** it; however, you now have the option to **Edit in Browser**. Click this menu tab to see how it works.

6. If prompted, **Sign in** by providing your SkyDrive credentials.

7. Once signed in, when a user clicks **Edit Document** two options are provided: **Edit in Word** and **Edit in Word Web App**. Either option allows the user to make changes to the Word document on your SkyDrive.

8. When you've finished exploring shared editing of your file, in the upper-right corner click **Sign Out**. Switch back to Word 2013.

9. To revoke a link's access to your file, click the **Disable Link** button. This permanently removes the link. Once disabled, it is gone! It will no longer work and you cannot restore it, but you can generate a new one. To conclude this demonstration, revoke both links by clicking each of the **Disable Link** buttons.

Note: You can generate similar links for users to access complete folders on your SkyDrive. This must be done from within SkyDrive. After logging into http://www.skydrive.com, simply check the box to select the file or folder you want to share, then from the menu across the top of the screen select either **Share>Get a Link** or select **Embed.**

Demonstration – Posting a Document to Facebook

1. This demonstration requires that you have completed the previous **Demonstration – Sharing a Document on SkyDrive**. You must also have a Facebook account. When you are connected to a file on SkyDrive, two new options will appear in Word 2013 under **File>Share**: **Get a Sharing Link** (or **Get a Link**) and **Post to Social Networks**. Select **Post to Social Networks**.

2. What you now see in the right pane depends on what you selected when you setup your online Microsoft Account. Connectors to the following social networks are currently available for Office 2013: **Facebook, Twitter, LinkedIn, Flickr,** and **Google**. If your Microsoft account is connected to one or more of these networks, their icons appear in the right pane with a checkbox next to each icon. If **Facebook** is in the right pane, skip to step 10.

3. If you are not yet connected to any social networks, press the link **Click here to connect social networks** and then skip to step 5.

4. If one or more social networks appear in the right pane, but not Facebook. Go to the upper-right corner of the screen and click your name to open the drop-down menu. Click **About Me**. If prompted, **Sign in** to your Microsoft Account using your SkyDrive credentials. Under your name and photo, click **Connect** to open your online Microsoft Account.

5. The **Add Accounts** page will list the social networks that have not yet been added, but are available to your Microsoft Account. Click **Facebook**.

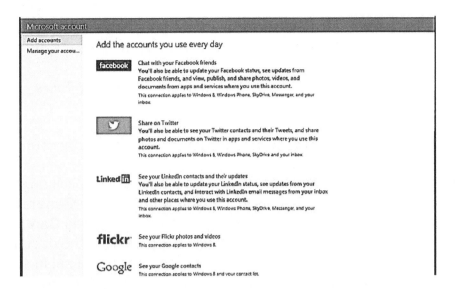

6. On the next page, click **Connect**. Login to your Facebook account.

7. On the Facebook **Request for Permission** page, click **Allow**. On the next page, click **Done**.

8. In the upper-right corner, click your name and **Sign out**.

9. Switch back to Word 2013, select **Post to Social Networks**. In the right pane, click the **Refresh** button. The Facebook logo should appear in the right pane.

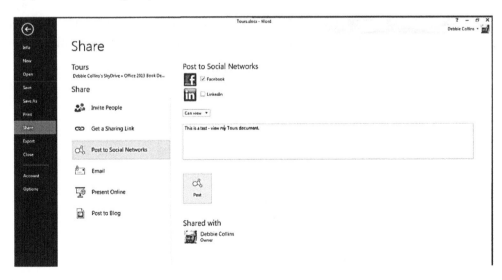

10. Enable the checkbox next to the **Facebook** logo. Select the permission level to grant to your file: **Can View** or **Can Edit.**

11. Type in the message field, *This is a test – View my Tours document*. Click the **Post** button.

12. Go to **http://www.facebook.com** and login to your account.

13. Your post should appear on your Facebook wall. Click on the **Sales** link to test it. Just as in the **Demonstration – Generating a Sharing Link**, if the permission you set in step 10 was **Can View**, you should be able to **Download** and **Find** items in the document, but not **Share** or edit anything. If the permission you set in step 10 was **Can Edit**, you should also have the option to **Edit in Browser**.

14. When you're finished testing your link, return to Word 2013, **File>Share>Post to Social Networks**. In the right pane, under **Shared With**, right-click the Facebook icon. Select **Disable Posted Link.** It will be removed from Word 2013.

15. Return to your Facebook wall. Hover in the upper-right corner of your post to reveal the option to **Edit or Delete**. Click it. Select **Delete...** In the next dialog box click **Delete**.

16. Your post on Facebook should be removed, but your connection between Office 2013 and Facebook is still active for other demonstrations in this book.

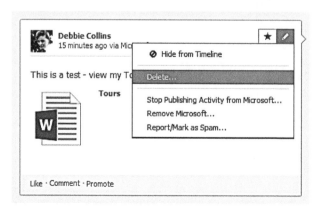

Simple Markup

Another feature to support collaboration is **Simple Markup**. This new tracking option provides a clean view of your document with red-line indicators appearing along the left margin to mark paragraphs and lines where tracked changes have been made. If you want to see the details of the changes, simply click the red-line indicator and the tracking option will automatically switch into **All Markup** so you can view the change details.

Lock Tracking

Have you ever shared a document for editing only to discover that one of your reviewers turned off tracking? This makes it very difficult to see what specific changes they made. Word 2013 solves this problem. If you want to prevent reviewers from accidently turning off tracking their changes, you can **Lock Tracking** with a password.

Demonstration – Simplified Markup and Lock Tracking

1. If you just completed a previous demonstration in this chapter, skip this step. Otherwise, in Word 2013 select **File>Open**. Select the location where you unzipped the demonstration files you downloaded in Chapter One (i.e., SkyDrive or Computer). **Browse** to *Tours.docx*. Select it and click the **Open** button.

2. Select the **Review** tab. Examine the **Tracking** group. Notice that **Simple Markup** is the default setting.

3. Click the **Tracking** button. There are now two options: **Track Changes** and **Lock Tracking**. Select **Lock Tracking** and provide a password. Click **OK**.

   Note: The configuration options which were under the **Track Changes** button in Word 2010 have been relocated. Click the **Change Tracking Options** dialog box launcher (arrow in the lower right corner of the **Tracking** group) to access them.

4. With **Track Changes** enabled, you are now ready to experience **Simple Markup**. In the first paragraph, replace the term *vacation* with *holiday*. Notice the red-line indicator in the left margin.

5. Click on the red-line indicator. Notice the tracking option automatically changes to **All Markup** and the details of the edit are displayed within the text of the document.

6. Leave the document in this status for the next demonstration.

Reply to Comment

Comments have been redesigned and now provide powerful collaboration capabilities. A **Reply** button has been added to the upper-right of the **Comment** balloon which allows reviewers to comment about comments! The owner of each comment is identified by name and, if available, a photo. Hover over the photo and the commenter's **Contact Card** is displayed. Click the arrow in the lower right to **Open Contact Card** and display the commenter's address, phone number, email address and other information pulled from the commenter's SkyDrive profile.

From the commenter's **Contact Card** you can click icons to communicate by **Instant Messenger, Phone**, or **Video**, or learn more about the commenter via their latest social updates. You can even click a link to schedule a meeting with the commenter using Outlook 2013!

When finished, instead of deleting a comment and losing it forever, you can now **Mark Comment Done**. The comment will fade to gray; yet remain if you need to refer to it in the future.

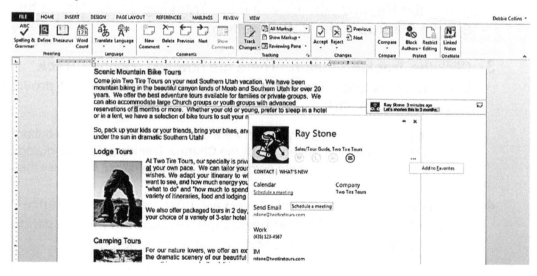

Demonstration – Reply to Comment

1. If you just completed a previous demonstration in this chapter, skip this step. Otherwise, in Word 2013 select **File>Open**. Select the location where you unzipped the demonstration files you downloaded in Chapter One (i.e., SkyDrive or Computer). **Browse** to *Tours.docx*. Select it and click the **Open** button.

2. Select the **Review** tab. If the **Tracking** option is set to **Simple Markup**, click the first comment icon located in the right margin of the first paragraph to open it. If **Tracking** is set to **All Markup,** the comment will already be open.

3. Click on the Reply icon located in the upper-right of the first comment. Type a reply, "I agree with Ray."

4. Hover over the photo in the comment to display the **Contact Card**.

   Note: If you don't see a bicycle as Ray's photo, you must **Sign In** to your SkyDrive account. Unless you are connected to SkyDrive, you will not see any information in the commenters **Contact Card**. Go to the upper-right corner of Word and click **Sign In**. Click the default option, **Microsoft Account**. Enter your credentials and click the **Sign In** button.

5. In the lower right corner of Ray's Contact Card, click the arrow icon **Open Contact Card**. Notice the four contact icons just below Ray's title. They are for **Instant Messenger, Phone**, **Video,** and **Social Network Status Updates**. Under the word **Calendar** is a link, **Schedule a meeting**, which opens Outlook 2013.

6. **Right-click** the photo in Ray's comment to open a short list of options. Click **Mark Comment Done**. It will turn gray and no longer display the Contact Card when the photo is selected. Right-click and disable **Mark Comments Done** to reactivate the comment.

Presenting Online

What if you don't have Lync or any other kind of web conferencing software, but you want to share your document with others as you read through it during a typical conference call? With Word 2013, you can send people a link to the document similar to the way you could in PowerPoint 2010. As you read through the Word document on your screen, your invitees can follow along in their browsers.   They don't even need Word!

Demonstration – Presenting Online

1. If you just completed a previous demonstration in this chapter, skip this step. Otherwise, in Word 2013 select **File>Open**. Select the location where you unzipped the demonstration files you downloaded in Chapter One (i.e., SkyDrive or Computer). **Browse** to *Tours.docx*. Select it and click the **Open** button.

2. If you just completed the previous demonstration, select the **Review** tab and disable **Lock Tracking** and **Track Changes**. Also, change the **Tracking** option back to **Simple Markup**.

3. Select **File>Share**. Select **Present Online.** Click the button, **Present Online**. A link will be generated for you to send to others.

    Note: If you're not signed in to your Microsoft (SkyDrive) account, you will be prompted to connect before you can proceed with **Present Online**.

4. Two options are available: **Copy Link** or **Send in Email**. If you **Copy Link**, you can paste it into an Instant Message. If you choose to **Send in Email**, Outlook 2013 will open. The link will be embedded in the body of the message, simply add invitees and send the email.

5. Once you've sent the link to the invitees, click **Start Presentation** and begin your show. A new Ribbon will appear. On the Ribbon are six options: **Share Meeting Notes, Send Invitations, Edit, Resume Online Presentation, End Online Presentation** and **Find**. Take a few moments to explore each of these options.

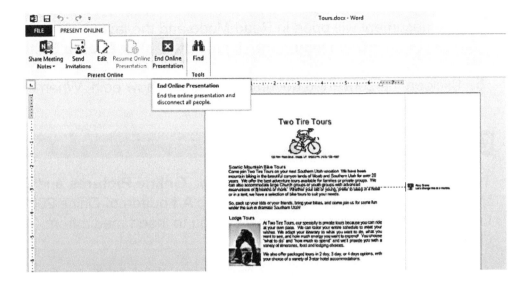

6. When finished exploring the options, click **End Online Presentation**. You will be returned to the **Print Layout** view of the document.

PDF Reflow

One of the most exciting new features of Word 2013 is the ability to open a PDF document and edit its content. The new PDF reflow feature works so well that you get a Word document that looks like the original PDF - complete with fonts, layout, images, tables, charts and page numbers – except it's all editable! Opening the PDF is so fast that it takes only a few seconds longer than opening the document in Acrobat Reader.

Demonstration – Opening a PDF for Editing

1. If you just completed a previous demonstration, close the document.

2. In Word 2013 select **File>Open**. Select the location where you unzipped the demonstration files you downloaded in Chapter One (i.e., SkyDrive or Computer). **Browse** to *Tours.pdf*. Select it and click the **Open** button.

3. If a dialog box pops up and warns that the conversion process may distort the placement of graphics, just click **OK**.

4. The document will open in Read Mode and the layout will look bad. Select **View>Edit Document**. If prompted, click **Enable Editing**.

5. Click on the converted document. You can now edit! When finished, select the **File** tab, and then click **Close**.

Online Media

Two new buttons appear on the Insert tab: **Online Pictures** and **Online Video**. **Online Pictures** replaces the Clip Art button of Office 2007 and Office 2010. Both online buttons allow you to insert media from Office.com or any source on the Internet.

To playback video in Word 2013 requires one of the following browsers:

- Internet Explorer 9 with at least the MS12-037: Cumulative Security Update for Internet Explorer: June 12, 2012 installed

- Or, Internet Explorer 10

Source: http://office.microsoft.com/en-us/support/supported-browsers-in-office-HA102789344.aspx

Demonstration – Inserting Online Pictures and Video

1. In Word 2013 select **File>Open**. Select the location where you unzipped the demonstration files you downloaded in Chapter One (i.e., SkyDrive or Computer). **Browse** to *Tours.docx*. Select it and click the **Open** button.

2. On the last page of the document, put your cursor at the end of the email address and press the enter key to allow room for a picture.

3. On the **Insert** tab, click **Online Pictures**. In the **Office.com Clip Art** field enter, *Mountain Biker*. Choose a photo and click **Insert**.

4. Above the Ribbon, on the **Quick Access Toolbar**, click the **Undo** button to delete the picture.

5. On the **Insert** tab, click **Online Video**. In the **Bing Video Search** field enter, *Slickrock Trail*. Choose a video and click **Insert**.

6. Leave the document open for the next demonstration.

Layout Options and Alignment Guides

Layout Options

Select a chart, image, shape, video, or SmartArt, and a button will appear in the upper-right of the object containing text wrapping options. These options are the same as in Office 2007 and Office 2010; however, you can now access them from the selected object. As you move, resize, or rotate the object, text reflows around it and appears as it would in its final position. When you've completed the move, the object and its surrounding text stay in that position. Microsoft calls this "Live Layout".

Alignment Guides

Whenever you start to drag a chart, image, shape, video, or SmartArt towards the edge or center of a document, a guide will appear to mark the vertical center, the horizontal center, or margins on the page. The purpose of these guides is to help you place objects onto your document.

Demonstration – Layout Options and Alignment Guides

1. Complete **Demonstration – Inserting Online Pictures and Video** prior to attempting this demonstration.

2. Select the video you inserted in the previous demonstration. Notice the **Layout Options** button that appears to the right. This is a new and quick alternative to using the **Wrap Text** button located on the **Picture Tools Format** tab. Select **Top and Bottom** text wrap.

3. Select the video again. Notice the green Alignment Guide marking the left margin. Drag the video around on the document and notice Alignment Guides appear and disappear marking the left margin, right margin, top and bottom margins, and center of the document.

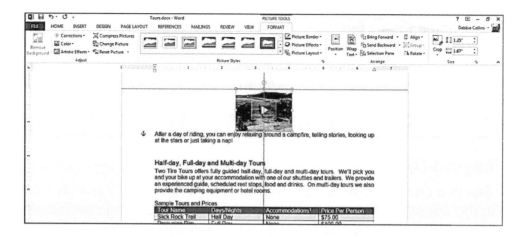

4. When finished exploring, drag the video back to its original place or delete it.

Working with Tables

Table management is easier in Word 2013. You can now add a new row or column with a single click. Other new features are **Border Styles** and a **Border Painter**. **Border Painter** allows you to choose a Border Style then apply it to a table by brushing it into place.

Demonstration – Adding Rows, Styles, and Borders

1. If you just completed the previous demonstration, skip this step. Otherwise, in Word 2013 select **File>Open**. Select the location where you unzipped the demonstration files you downloaded in Chapter One (i.e., SkyDrive or Computer). **Browse** to *Tours.docx*. Select it and click the **Open** button.

2. On the last page of the document, move your cursor along the left border of the table. The little plus (+) symbol is the **Add Row** icon. If you move your cursor along the top border of the table, this symbol is the **Add Column** icon.

3. Place the icon between the **Porcupine Rim** and **Canyonlands** rows. Click the (+) icon to add a blank row.

4. Type into the new blank row, *Bartlett Wash   Full Day   None $100.00*

5. Select **Table Tools>Design** and open the **Table Styles** gallery. Unlike Word 2010, these styles are organized into three groups: **Plain Tables, Grid Tables** and **List Tables**.

6. In the group to the right of the **Table Styles** gallery are two new tools for working with table borders: **Border Styles** and **Border Painter**. Click **Border Styles** and on the second row, third column, select **Single solid line, 1 1/2 pt, Accent 2**. Notice the **Border Painter** automatically enables.

7. Paint this new border down each of the three inside column lines and around the four outside borders of the table. Remember, you can enlarge the table using the **Zoom** slider in the lower right corner of the screen to make it more comfortable to see the lines.

8. Click **Border Painter** to deactivate it.

WordArt

The **WordArt** tool in Word 2013 is almost identical to the tool found in Word 2010 and PowerPoint 2010; however, it is very different from the **WordArt** that existed in Word 2003/2007. If you're familiar with WordArt in Word 2010, you know that the tool allows you to do more than simply apply a **WordArt** style. It also allows you to manipulate text effects, fills and outlines. The major difference between WordArt in Word 2013 versus Word 2010 is the available **WordArt Styles** (predefined combinations) were reduced from thirty (30) in Word 2010 to fifteen (15) in Word 2013.

Demonstration – Adding WordArt

1. If you just completed a previous demonstration in this chapter, skip this step. Otherwise, in Word 2013 select **File>Open**. Select the location where you unzipped the demonstration files you downloaded in Chapter One (i.e., SkyDrive or Computer). **Browse** to *Tours.docx*. Select it and click the **Open** button.

2. On the last page, below all the other content, press your Enter key a few times to create some empty space and then type, *Let's Ride!*

3. Select the text, *Let's Ride!*

4. On the **Insert** tab, click **WordArt** and select **Fill-Red, Accent 2, Outline-Accent 2**. If you don't have this specific color, select another color. Your text *Let's Ride!* will be converted to WordArt.

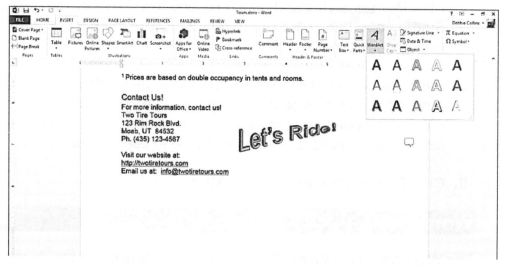

5. On the **Drawing Tools Format** tab, in the **Arrange** group, click **Align>Align Center**.

6. To the right of the **Word Styles** gallery, click **Text Effects** and select **Transform**. Scroll-down the **Warp** options to the second row from the bottom and select **Fade Right**.

7. Click **Text Effects** again and choose **3-D Rotation>Parallel**, select **Off Axis 1 Right**.

8. Click **Text Effects** again. Choose **Bevel>Bevel**, select **Cool Slant**.

9. Drag the WordArt to the right of the Contact Us text block.

Chapter Summary

This chapter examined the new features of Word 2013 using a hands-on approach. Read Mode, Object Zoom, Co-editing and Presenting Online were explored as new features supporting collaboration.

You learned that Word 2013 can edit PDF documents using PDF reflow. This new feature is used to convert a PDF document with text, tables, and graphics into Word format.

A few graphics enhancements were examined. Two new media buttons were explored called, Online Pictures and Online Video. You used these buttons to insert media onto a document. You discovered that a convenient Layout Options button is displayed to the right of an object whenever it's selected, and Alignment Guides appear whenever new objects are dragged around the page. Alignment Guides mark the margins and the center of the document to help you more accurately position items.

You managed a table with a new feature that allows you to add rows and columns more quickly, and you selected a Border Style and learned to apply it with the new Border Painter.

Finally, this chapter demonstrated the text effects that can be applied to WordArt.

Chapter 4: New Features of Excel 2013

This chapter covers the following topics:

- ✓ Co-editing
- ✓ New Functions
- ✓ Flash Fill
- ✓ Quick Analysis Tool
- ✓ Recommended Charts
- ✓ Chart Formatting Control
- ✓ Chart Animation
- ✓ Recommended Pivot Tables
- ✓ Timeline Filter
- ✓ Power View and PowerPivot
- ✓ Inquire Add-in

Some of the most noticeable enhancements made to Office 2013 are found in Excel. Collaboration capabilities have been enhanced and new functions have been added; however, the majority of improvements focus on making advanced charting and tables friendlier to mainstream users.

This chapter begins with new features supporting collaboration. Several new Functions will be listed and Flash Fill will be explored. You will experience enhancements designed to make familiar tasks faster and easier, such as the Quick Analysis Tool, Recommended Charts, Chart Formatting Control, Chart Animation, Recommended Pivot Tables and Timeline Filters. This chapter concludes by examining three advanced features - Power View, PowerPivot and the Inquire add-in.

To master the new features presented in this chapter, you are encouraged to follow along with the hands-on demonstrations. You may use or create your own files; however, specific files are referenced in the instructions to help you master these features more quickly. Refer to Chapter One in this book for instructions on how to download the demonstration files.

Co-editing

The same steps used to share documents and collaborate in Word 2013, apply to spreadsheets and workbooks in Excel 2013. When saving a workbook to SkyDrive or SharePoint, the owner can choose who to share with and whether each invitee can view or edit the workbook. Just like in Excel 2010, the owner can also protect the workbook structure or restrict specific editing activity on a worksheet. After the Excel file is saved and the permissions are set, the owner can send the invitees an access link via email. Of course, the greatest advantage of collaborating within the cloud is that your invitees are assured they are seeing the latest version of your workbook. Excel 2013 also integrates with social networking sites by allowing you to embed a SkyDrive link on a blog or social network page that lets others view or edit your spreadsheet.

Users of a business or professional edition of Excel 2013 can also collaborate with others via Lync. With Lync, the owner can grant others in a conversation or meeting live control of the workbook so collaboration across distance is easier than ever before.

Share

Sharing an Excel 2013 workbook on SkyDrive was introduced in Office 2010, but in Office 2013 it's simpler.

Under the **File** tab in the **Backstage** view of Excel 2013 is a new feature called, **Share**. This feature replaces Save & Send, which was in Office 2010. All of the options that were in Save & Send still exist in **Share**, and a few new ones have been added. The process is similar to sharing a Word 2013 document.

Demonstration – Sharing a Workbook on SkyDrive

1. In Excel 2013 select **File>Open**. Select the location where you unzipped the demonstration files you downloaded in Chapter One (i.e., SkyDrive or Computer). **Browse** to *Sales.xlsx*. Select it and click the **Open** button.

2. Select **File>Share**. Two options are displayed: **Invite People** and **Email**. Email is the same as it was in Excel 2010 under Save & Send. For this demonstration, select **Invite People**.

3. When **Invite People** is selected, a button will be displayed in the right pane called, **Save to Cloud**. Click it. This will actually take you to **File>Save As**. Three options are displayed under **Save As** which are: **SkyDrive**, **Computer** (i.e., local drive or network drive) and **Add a Place** (i.e., Office 365 SharePoint).

Note: A fourth option will display if you are signed into an Office 365 account, **Other Web Locations** (i.e., SharePoint or another online storage service).

4. Select **SkyDrive**. If you completed Chapter Three, you will see a **Browse** button in the right pane. If you see **Browse**, skip to step 7.

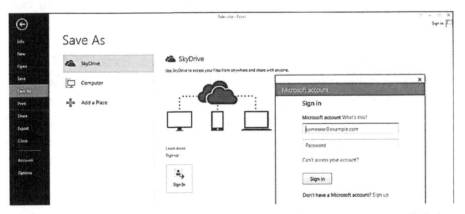

5. If instead of a **Browse** button you see a **Sign In** button, click it and provide the credentials you created when you setup your SkyDrive account in Chapter Two. This connects Office 2013 to your SkyDrive. If you did not create a SkyDrive account in Chapter Two, click the Sign up link and create an account first, then click **Sign In**.

6. When Excel 2013 is connected to your SkyDrive, its name will be displayed and you will be provided a button to **Browse** it

Note: If you later want to disconnect Excel 2013 from an online service, such as SkyDrive, go to the **File>Account** option. Below your photo, click **Sign Out**. Or, for other connections, choose the **Connected Service** from the list and click the **Remove** link. To reconnect to SkyDrive, repeat steps 3 thru 6 above.

7. Click the **Browse** button. This will open your SkyDrive.

8. Browse to the folder you created in Chapter Three that you named, *Office 2013 Book Demos*. If you did not create this folder in Chapter Three, create it now by clicking **New Folder.** Save your *Sales.xlsx* workbook into this SkyDrive folder.

9. After you save your workbook to SkyDrive, Excel 2013 will automatically return you to **Invite People**. In the top field, enter the email addresses of people with whom you want to share your workbook. You can validate the email addresses by clicking the first icon to the right of the name field. You can also choose names from your Outlook Address Book by clicking the second icon.

10. The drop-down menu to the right of the name field allows you to choose the file access you are granting this specific list of people: **Can view** or **Can edit.**

11. You can also include a message in your invitation by typing it into the message field.

12. When you have finished configuring your invitation, click the **Share** button. SkyDrive may prompt you for additional information. If so, click the link for additional authentication and follow the instructions. An email will automatically be sent to your invitees that includes your message and link to your workbook. Your list of invitees displays under **Shared With** so you'll always know who can access this file.

Get a Sharing Link and Post to Social Networks

Permission to view or edit files on SkyDrive is embedded in the access link provided to a viewer. Once a workbook has been placed onto SkyDrive, you share it by sending others either a link to view, or a link to edit.

If you want your invitees to be identified on the workbook's **Share** pane, use **Invite People** to generate the access links. If listing each individual's identity on the **Share** pane is not important and you'd rather have the convenience of inviting people by group, you can **Get a Sharing Link** and send it in a bulk email. Another way to share with groups of people is to embed a link onto a web page, blog, or post it on a social networking site.

Demonstration – Generating a Sharing Link

1. This demonstration requires that you complete the previous **Demonstration – Sharing a Workbook on SkyDrive**. When you are connected to a workbook on SkyDrive, two new options will appear in Excel 2013 under **File>Share**: **Get a Sharing Link** (or **Get a Link**) and **Post to Social Networks**. Select **Get a Sharing Link** (or **Get a Link**).

2. In the right pane are two fields: **View Link** and **Edit Link**. To the right of each of these empty fields is a button, **Create Link**. Click each of these buttons to generate the two types of links.

3. After generating the type of link you want, simply copy the link and paste it into a group email or onto a web page. Anyone who clicks the link will be taken to your workbook and have the level of access specified by the link. At the bottom of the pane, under **Shared With,** the links are listed to remind you of their existence for this workbook.

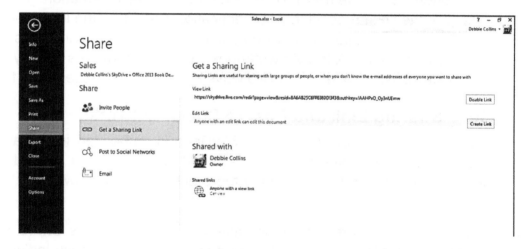

4. To test your links, copy the **View Link** you generated and paste it into your browser. This opens the workbook on SkyDrive. Notice that you can **Download** and **Find** items within the workbook, but you cannot **Share** it, nor edit anything. You have View access only.

5. Next, copy the **Edit Link** and paste it into your browser. Just like with View permission, you can **Download** and **Find** items in the workbook, but you cannot **Share** it; however, you now have the option to **Edit in Browser**. Click this menu tab to see how it works.

6. If prompted, **Sign in** by providing your SkyDrive credentials.

7. Once signed in, when a user clicks **Edit Workbook** two options are provided: **Edit in Excel** and **Edit in Excel Web App**. Either option allows the user to make changes to the workbook on your SkyDrive.

8. When you've finished exploring shared editing of your workbook, in the upper-right corner click **Sign Out**. Switch back to Excel 2013.

9. To revoke a link's access to your workbook, click the **Disable Link** button. This permanently removes the link. Once disabled, it is gone! It will no longer work and you cannot restore it, but you can generate a new one. To conclude this demonstration, revoke both links by clicking each of the **Disable Link** buttons.

Note: You can generate similar links for users to access complete folders on your SkyDrive. This must be done from within SkyDrive. After logging into http://www.skydrive.com, simply check the box to select the file or folder you want to share, then from the menu across the top of the screen select either **Share>Get a Link** or select **Embed**.

Demonstration – Posting a Workbook to Facebook

1. This demonstration requires that you complete the previous **Demonstration – Sharing a Workbook on SkyDrive**. You must also have a Facebook account. When you are connected to a workbook on SkyDrive, two new options will appear in Excel 2013 under **File>Share**: **Get a Sharing Link** (or **Get a Link**) and **Post to Social Networks**. Select **Post to Social Networks**.

2. What you now see in the right pane depends on what you selected when you setup your online Microsoft Account. Connectors to the following social networks are currently available for Office 2013: **Facebook, Twitter, LinkedIn, Flickr,** and **Google**. If your Microsoft

account is connected to one or more of these networks, their icons appear in the right pane with a checkbox next to each icon. If **Facebook** is in the right pane, skip to step 10.

3. If you are not yet connected to any social networks, press the link **Click here to connect social networks** and then skip to step 5.

4. If one or more social networks appear in the right pane, but not Facebook. Go to the upper-right corner of the screen and click your name to open the drop-down menu. Click **About Me**. If prompted, **Sign in** to your Microsoft Account using your SkyDrive credentials. Under your name and photo, click **Connect** to open your online Microsoft Account.

5. The **Add Accounts** page will list the social networks that have not yet been added, but are available to your Microsoft Account. Click **Facebook**.

6. On the next page, click **Connect**. Login to your Facebook account.

7. On the Facebook's **Request for Permission** page, click **Allow**. On the next page, click **Done**.

8. In the upper-right corner, click your name and **Sign out**.

9. Switch back to Excel 2013, select **Post to Social Networks**. In the right pane, click the **Refresh** button. The Facebook logo should appear in the right pane.

10. Enable the checkbox next to the **Facebook** logo. Select the permission level to grant to your file: **Can View** or **Can Edit**.

11. Type the message, *This is a test – View my Sales workbook.*

12. Click the **Post** button.

13. Go to **http://www.facebook.com** and login to your account.

14. Your post should appear on your Facebook wall. Click on the **Sales** link to test it. Just as in the **Demonstration – Generating a Sharing Link**, if the permission you set in step 10 was **Can View**, you should be able to **Download** and **Find** items in the workbook, but not **Share** or edit anything. If the permission you set in step 10 was **Can Edit**, you should also have the option to **Edit in Browser**.

15. When you're finished testing your link, return to Excel 2013, **File>Share>Post to Social Networks**. In the right pane, under **Shared With**, right-click the Facebook icon. Select **Disable Posted Link.** It will be removed from Excel 2013.

16. Return to your Facebook wall. Hover in the upper-right corner of your post to reveal the option to **Edit or Delete**. Click it. Select **Delete...** In the next dialog box click **Delete**.

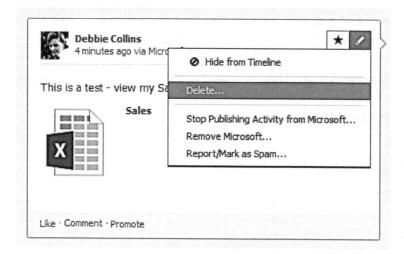

17. Your post on Facebook should be removed, but your connection between Office 2013 and Facebook is still active for other demonstrations in this book.

New Functions

Excel 2013 has forty-eight new functions that were not available in previous versions, plus two functions that have been moved to another category and two functions that have been renamed. These are listed on the Formulas tab in the Function Library under the following categories: Date & Time, Engineering, Financial, Information, Logical, Lookup & Reference, Math & Trig, Statistical, Text and Web.

The following table lists all of the functions that are new, moved or renamed, in Excel 2013:

Table 4. New, Moved or Renamed Functions in Excel 2013

Category	Function	Explanation
Compatibility	CEILING (previously in Math & Trig)	Rounds a number up to the nearest multiple of significance.
Compatibility	FLOOR (previously in Math & Trig)	Rounds a number down to the nearest multiple of significance.
Date and time	DAYS	Returns the number of days between two dates.
Date and time	ISOWEEKNUM	Returns number of the ISO week number of the year for a given date.
Engineering	BITAND	Returns a bitwise "And' of two numbers.
Engineering	BITLSHIFT	Returns a number shifted left by shift_amount bits.
Engineering	BITOR	Returns a bitwise "Or" of two numbers.
Engineering	BITRSHIFT	Returns a number shifted right by shift_amount bits.
Engineering	BITXOR	Returns a bitwise 'Exclusive Or' of two numbers.
Engineering	IMCOSH	Returns the hyperbolic cosine of a complex number.
Engineering	IMCOT	Returns the cotangent of a complex number.
Engineering	IMCSC	Returns the cosecant of a complex number.
Engineering	IMCSCH	Returns the hyperbolic cosecant of a complex number.
Engineering	IMSEC	Returns the secant of a complex number.
Engineering	IMSECH	Returns the hyperbolic secant of a complex number.
Engineering	IMSINH	Returns the hyperbolic sine of a complex number.
Engineering	IMTAN	Returns the tangent of a complex number.
Financial	PDURATION	Returns the number of periods required by an investment to reach a specified value.
Financial	RRI	Returns an equivalent interest rate for the growth of an investment.
Information	ISFORMULA	Checks whether a reference is to a cell containing a formula, and returns TRUE or FALSE.
Information	SHEET	Returns the sheet number of the referenced sheet.

Information	SHEETS	Returns the number of sheets in a reference.
Logical	IFNA	Returns the value you specify if the expression resolves to #N/A, otherwise returns the result of the expression.
Logical	XOR	Returns a logical "Exclusive Or" of all arguments.
Lookup & Reference	FORMULATEXT	Returns a formula as a string.
Math & Trig	ACOT	Returns the arc cotangent of a number, in radians in the range 0 to Pi.
Math & Trig	ACOTH	Returns the inverse hyperbolic arc cotangent of a number.
Math & Trig	ARABIC	Converts a Roman numeral to Arabic.
Math & Trig	BASE	Converts a number into a text representation with the given radix (base).
Math & Trig	CEILING.MATH (previous named CEILING.PRECISE)	Rounds a number up, to the nearest integer or to the nearest multiple of significance.
Math & Trig	COMBINA	Returns the number of combinations with repetitions for a given number of items.
Math & Trig	COT	Returns the cotangent of an angle.
Math & Trig	COTH	Returns the hyperbolic cotangent of a number.
Math & Trig	CSC	Returns the cosecant of an angle.
Math & Trig	CSCH	Returns the hyperbolic cosecant of an angle.
Math & Trig	DECIMAL	Converts a text representation of a number in a given base into a decimal number.
Math & Trig	FLOOR.MATH (previously named FLOOR.PRECISE)	Rounds a number down, to the nearest integer or to the nearest multiple of significance
Math & Trig	MUNIT	Returns the unit matrix for the specified dimension.
Math & Trig	SEC	Returns the secant of an angle.
Math & Trig	SECH	Returns the hyperbolic secant of an angle.
Statistical	BINOM.DIST.RANGE	Returns the probability of a trial result using a binomial distribution.
Statistical	GAMMA	Returns the Gamma function value.
Statistical	GAUSS	Returns 0.5 less than the standard normal cumulative distribution.

Statistical	PERMUTATIONA	Returns the number of permutations for a given number of objects (with repetitions) that can be selected from the total objects.
Statistical	PHI	Returns the value of the density function for a standard normal distribution.
Statistical	SKEW.P	Returns the skewness of a distribution based on a population: a characterization of the degree of asymmetry of a distribution around its mean.
Text	NUMBERVALUE	Converts text to number in a locale-independent manner.
Text	UNICHAR	Returns the Unicode character that is referenced by the given numeric value
Text	UNICODE	Returns the number (code point) corresponding to the first character of the text.
Web	ENCODEURL	Returns a URL-encoded string
Web	FILTERXML	Returns specific data from the XML content by using the specified XPath.
Web	WEBSERVICE	Returns data from a web service.

Flash Fill

If you liked Auto fill in earlier versions of Excel, you're going to love "Flash Fill" in Excel 2013. This new feature reads patterns in adjacent columns looking for similar formulas and formatting. The user simply begins filling data into a new column and clicks Flash Fill. If a pattern is recognized from adjacent columns, Excel automatically completes the remaining entries in the new column. No macros required! Flash Fill can extract or concatenate (join) data, reverse last and first names, insert letters or symbols or numbers, and speed up many other tasks that were before tedious. This is one of the most time-saving features of Excel 2013!

Demonstration – Flash Fill

1. If you just completed a previous demonstration in this chapter, skip this step. Otherwise, in Excel 2013 select **File>Open**. Select the location where you unzipped the demonstration files downloaded in Chapter One (i.e., SkyDrive or Computer). **Browse** to *Sales.xlsx*. Select it and click the **Open** button.

2. On the *Sales.xlsx* workbook, select the **Tours Booked** tab.

3. In the **Booking Reference** column, cell **K6**, type the following text with 5 spaces after each comma, then press the **Enter key**:

Customer: L. Davis,   Size: 11,   Length: 4-Day/3-Night

4. Select the **Data** tab. In the **Data Tools** group, click the **Flash Fill** button. Or, from the **Home** tab, **Editing** group, click **Fill>Flash Fill**. Or, use the short-cut key **CTRL+E.** Excel completes the column!

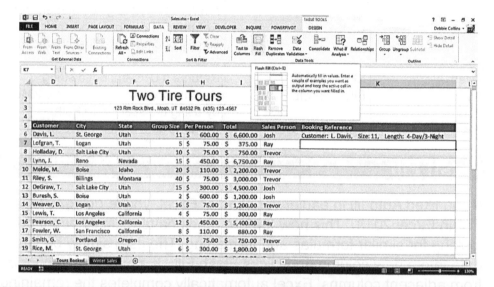

Quick Analysis Tool

When a user selects a range of data on a spreadsheet, Excel 2013 pops up a box in the lower-right of the selection containing "Quick Analysis" options. The options are a recommended set of analytic actions that offer a live preview of the data if one or more of the following are applied:

- **Formatting** - Color Scales, Data Bar, Icon Set, and more;
- **Charts** – Excel 2013 will recommend the most appropriate display;
- **Totals** – Sum, Average, Count, % of Total, and others;
- **Tables** – Simple tables and PivotTable variations;
- **Sparklines** – Line, Column, and Win/Loss

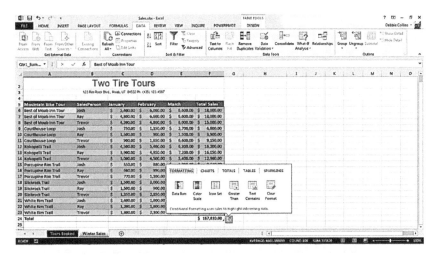

Of course, these five options are not new to Excel and existed in previous versions. The Quick Analysis tool simply makes them more accessible with a single click and offers a live preview of what will result!

Demonstration – Quick Analysis Tool

1. If you just completed a previous demonstration in this chapter, skip this step. Otherwise, in Excel 2013 select **File>Open**. Select the location where you unzipped the demonstration files downloaded in Chapter One (i.e., SkyDrive or Computer). **Browse** to *Sales.xlsx*. Select it and click the **Open** button.

2. On the *Sales.xlsx* workbook, select the **Winter Sales** tab.

3. Select cells **A6:F23**. Click the **Quick Analysis Tool** in the lower right corner of the table. The five options listed above are displayed.

4. Explore the options, if you'd like. The options are the same as they were in Excel 2010.

Recommended Charts

Excel 2013 can recognize patterns in your data and suggest charts that best illustrate those patterns. This feature is accessed from a button on the **Insert** tab called **Recommended Charts**.

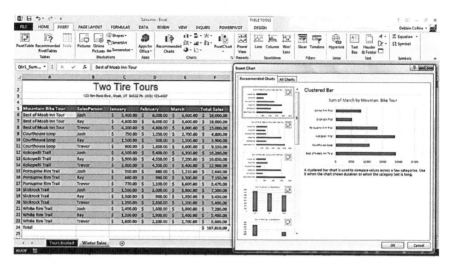

The top recommended charts can also be accessed from the Charts option on the Quick Analysis Tool; however, for the most comprehensive list use the button on the Insert tab.

Excel 2013 will display a list of chart thumbnails already populated with your data!

Demonstration – Recommended Charts

1. If you just completed a previous demonstration in this chapter, skip this step. Otherwise, in Excel 2013 select **File>Open**. Select the location where you unzipped the demonstration files downloaded in Chapter One (i.e., SkyDrive or Computer). **Browse** to *Sales.xlsx*. Select it and click the **Open** button.

2. On the *Sales.xlsx* workbook, select the **Winter Sales** tab.

3. Select cells **A6:F23**. On the **Insert** tab, in the **Charts** group, click the **Recommended Charts** button.

4. Hover down the list on the **Recommended Charts** tab. Notice they are all live preview, already populated with your data! Also, explore the charts on the **All Charts** tab.

   Note: Charts identified with an icon of a curved arrow in their upper-right corner are PivotCharts.

5. Select a pivot chart, such as **Recommended Chart**, **Clustered Bar**, **Sum of Total Sales by Mountain Bike Tour** and click **OK**. This PivotChart and its PivotTable will be inserted onto a new page.

6. On the **Winter Sales** tab, select **A6:F23** again. On the **Insert** tab, in the **Charts** group, click the **Recommended Charts** button again. Scroll down the list and select the very colorful **Clustered Column** chart. Click **OK**. Drag the chart and position it to the left of the table.

Chart Formatting Control

Formatting charts in Excel 2013 is now quicker. When a chart is selected, three new option boxes appear to the right of the chart – **Chart Elements**, **Styles/Colors**, and **Filters**. Within each of these boxes are thumbnails that offer live previews of your data if the options are applied. This new feature of Chart Formatting makes it quicker and easier to change the title, layout, color, style, and other elements of your chart.

Demonstration – Chart Formatting

1. This demonstration requires that you complete the previous **Demonstration – Recommended Charts**. Select the last chart you created in that demonstration called, **Clustered Column** chart. Three icons will appear on the right side of the chart. You may need to scroll the view horizontally to see them.

2. Click the **first icon** that looks like a **Plus** symbol. This tool lets you turn on and off **Chart Elements** by selecting the checkbox. Hover over each element to see a live preview. Click the arrow to the right of one of the elements to open its Options list. Explore these. On one of the Options lists, click **More Options** to open the side panel which allows you precise formatting control over the element.

3. Click the **second icon** that looks like a **Paintbrush** symbol. This lets you change **Chart Styles** by selecting the appropriate tab. Hover over each style or color set to see a live preview of the effect.

4. Click the **third icon** that is the **Chart Filters** symbol. This lets you choose which data from the table to display on the chart. Clear **Series1, Series2 and Series3**. Leave only **Series4** enabled.

Chart Animation

If you change a data entry in a chart's table, you will see the affect immediately with another new feature Microsoft calls, "Chart Animation". When you change the table data, Excel's chart engine animates that portion of the chart to show how the new number affects the visualization. Even the scale of the axes can change to match!

Demonstration – Chart Animation

1. This demonstration requires that you complete the previous **Demonstration – Chart Formatting.** Select the chart you just formatted called, **Clustered Column** chart.

2. On the table in cell **D10**, change the value **$900** to **$9,000** and notice the change in the column is animated. Change it back to **$900** and observe the animation again.

Recommended PivotTables

Another new button on the **Insert** tab is "Recommended PivotTables". A list of PivotTables can also be found under the **Tables** tab in the **Quick Analysis** toolbox. Just like with Recommended Charts, the gallery of PivotTables is pre-populated with a live preview of your data so you can choose the PivotTable that best communicates your results.

Demonstration – Recommended PivotTables

1. If you just completed a previous demonstration in this chapter, skip this step. Otherwise, in Excel 2013 select **File>Open**. Select the location where you unzipped the demonstration files downloaded in Chapter One (i.e., SkyDrive or Computer). **Browse** to *Sales.xlsx*. Select it and click the **Open** button.

2. On the *Sales.xlsx* workbook, select the **Winter Sales** tab.

3. Select cells **A6:F23**. On the **Insert** tab, in the **Tables** group, click the **Recommended PivotTables** button.

4. Click down the list of **Recommended PivotTables**. Notice they are all live preview, already populated with your data!

5. Select the fifth **Recommended PivotTable**, **Sum of Total Sales** (the first table that lists the Mountain Bike Tours). Click **OK**. The PivotTable will be inserted onto a new page.

Timeline Filter

Would you like to compare your PivotTable or PivotChart data over different time periods? Instead of regrouping your data by dates, you can now filter data as it occurs over sequential time periods such as daily, monthly, quarterly or yearly.

Whenever a PivotChart or PivotTable is selected, tool tabs appear on the Ribbon. These contextual tabs are **Analyze** and **Design** (PivotCharts also has a shape **Format** tab). The **Analyze** tab in Excel 2013 replaces the former PivotChart Options and PivotTable Options tab from previous versions of Excel.

The new **Insert Timeline** feature is located in the **Filter** group of the **Analyze** tab.

Demonstration – Using Timeline

1. If you just completed a previous demonstration in this chapter, skip this step. Otherwise, in Excel 2013 select **File>Open**. Select the location where you unzipped the demonstration files downloaded in Chapter One (i.e., SkyDrive or Computer). **Browse** to *Sales.xlsx*. Select it and click the **Open** button.

2. On the *Sales.xlsx* workbook, select the **Tours Booked** tab.

3. Select cells **A6:K40**. On the **Insert** tab, in the **Charts** group, click the **Recommended Charts** button.

4. Hover down the list on the **Recommended Charts** tab and choose the second chart, **Clustered Column, Sum of Total by State**.

5. The PivotChart and PivotTable will both be placed onto a new worksheet. Select either the **PivotChart** or the **PivotTable**.

6. On the **Analyze** tab, in the **Filter** group, click the **Insert Timeline**. Enable **Date**. Click **OK**.

7. Click on each month from **JAN 2012 to APR 2012** in the **Timeline** and watch the change occur on both the chart and table.

8. Click the **Period** menu in the upper-right corner of the **Timeline** to change the display to **Years, Quarters, Months,** or **Days**.

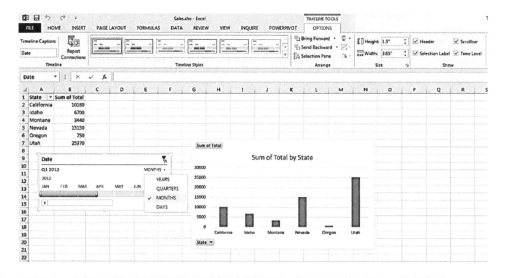

Power View

Many of the features that were in Power View for SharePoint 2010 are now integrated into Excel 2013 in the Office Professional Plus 2013 edition. Power View is a reporting tool that provides interactive data exploration, visualization, and presentation. With a Power View report, you can pull your data together in tables, matrices, maps, and charts in an interactive view that can bring your data to life.

Power View is included only in the Office Professional Plus 2013 edition. Some readers of this book won't have Office Professional Plus 2013, so won't be able to participate in the following demonstration.

In this demonstration we will use Power View and Bing to create a report that plots customer locations and sales onto a map.

Demonstration – Creating a Map Using Power View

1. If you just completed a previous demonstration in this chapter, skip this step. Otherwise, in Excel 2013 select **File>Open**. Select the location where you unzipped the demonstration files downloaded in Chapter One (i.e., SkyDrive or Computer). **Browse** to *Sales.xlsx*. Select it and click the **Open** button.

2. On the *Sales.xlsx* workbook, select the **Tours Booked** tab.

3. Select cells **A6:K40**, go to the **Insert** tab. Located in the center of the Ribbon, in the **Reports** group, click the **Power View** button. Wait a few moments while the Power View **Design** tab opens.

4. In the **Power View Fields** pane on the right, clear all the checkboxes except **City**, **State** and **Total** (make sure to select **Total**). On the left side of the **Design** tab, click on the **Map** button.

5. A yellow bar will appear across the top of the window warning you to enable content so the data can be sent to Bing to get geocoded. Click **Enable Content** to proceed (Internet connection is required).

6. Hover over the map, in the upper-right click **Pop Out** to enlarge it.

7. Arrange your fields by dragging **Total** into the **Size** field, **City** into the **Locations** field, and **City** into the **Color** field. The end result should be a map report which shows the cities as colored bubbles that differ in size depending on the amount of Total sales.

8. You can also play around with other properties like **Title, Legend, Data Labels** and **Map Background**. Buttons for these features are on the **Layout** tab.

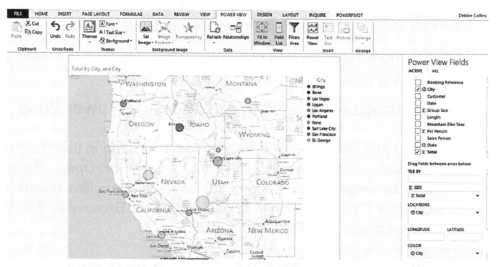

9. Right-click the worksheet tab and **Rename** it, *Power View Map*.

PowerPivot

The same PowerPivot add-in that enhanced the capabilities of Excel 2010, when combined with SharePoint 2010, is now natively integrated into Microsoft Office Professional Plus 2013; you simply need to enable it. Once enabled, the PowerPivot tab will appear on the Excel 2013 Ribbon.

PowerPivot is an advanced feature that allows you to build or modify data models. Use it to define your own Calculated Fields, Key Performance Indicators (KPIs), filter imported data, and Detect Relationships.

PowerPivot is included only in the Office Professional Plus 2013 edition. Some readers of this book won't have Office Professional Plus 2013, so won't be able to participate in the following demonstration.

Demonstration – Enabling the PowerPivot Tab

1. The PowerPivot add-in is available in Microsoft Office Professional Plus 2013. It is built into Excel 2013, you simply need to enable it. If

you just completed a previous demonstration in this chapter, skip this step. Otherwise, in Excel 2013 select **File>Open**. Select the location where you unzipped the demonstration files downloaded in Chapter One (i.e., SkyDrive or Computer). **Browse** to *Sales.xlsx*. Select it and click the **Open** button.

2. On the *Sales.xlsx* workbook, select the **Tours Booked** tab.

3. Select the **File** tab, select **Options**, and select **Add-Ins**.

4. At the bottom, in the Manage box, use the drop-down menu to change the selection to **COM Add-ins**. Click the **Go** button.

5. Check the box for **Microsoft Office PowerPivot for Excel 2013**, and then click **OK**. If you have previous versions of Excel installed, those versions of PowerPivot may also be listed in the COM Add-ins list. Be sure to select the PowerPivot add-in for Excel 2013.

6. The Ribbon should now have the **PowerPivot** tab.

Demonstration – Creating a Drill Down Capable Map

1. This is an enhancement to the **Demonstration – Creating a Map Using Power View**. It is recommended you complete the previous demonstration prior to this one so you can compare the differences.

2. On the *Sales.xlsx* workbook, select the **Tours Booked** tab.

3. Select cells **A6:K40**, go to the **PowerPivot** tab.

4. On the **PowerPivot** tab, click the **Add to Data Model** button. If prompted to create a table, click **OK**. A new window will open with a PowerPivot table that has the same content as your source table.

5. Within this new PowerPivot window, select the **Advanced** tab. You must now verify that PowerPivot recognizes your State and City fields as geographic entities. Do this by selecting the **City** column, then click the **Data Category** drop-down menu. City should display

with a checkmark. Repeat this step by selecting the **State** column and clicking on the **Data Category** drop-down menu. State should have a checkmark. These are separate lists, so they will not both have a checkmark in the same list.

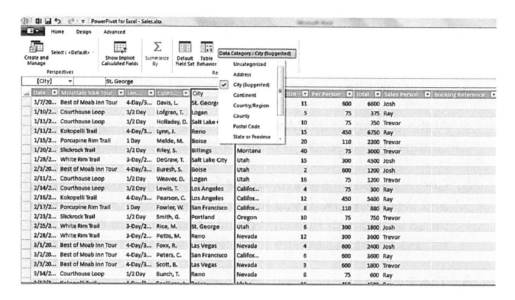

6. Now we will recreate the geographic map you made in the previous **Demonstration – Creating a Map Using Power View**. Except your new map will be interactive so you can drill down from State to City.

7. On the *Sales.xlsx* workbook, select the **Tours Booked** tab.

8. Select the entire table, go to the **Insert** tab. Located in the center of the Ribbon, in the **Reports** group, click the **Power View** button. You will be prompted how you want to create the Power View report. Select **Create a Power View Sheet**. Click **OK**.

9. On the new Power View worksheet, in the **Power View Fields** pane on the right, notice the City and State data objects now have a globe icon next to them where they did not in the previous demonstration.

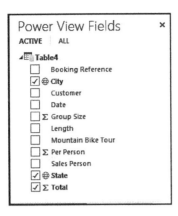

10. In the **Power View Fields** pane, make sure only **City**, **State** and **Total** are selected. The checkboxes for all other items should be cleared. On the left side of the **Design** tab, click on the **Map** button.

11. Hover over the map, in its upper-right corner click the **Pop Out** icon to enlarge the map.

12. Arrange your fields by dragging **Total** into the **Size** field, **City** and **State** into the **Locations** field, and **City** into the **Color** field. The end result should be a map report which shows the cities as colored bubbles that differ in size depending on the amount of Total sales.

13. Clear the checkbox, **City**. The map will reconfigure so there is only one bubble representing the Total sales in each State.

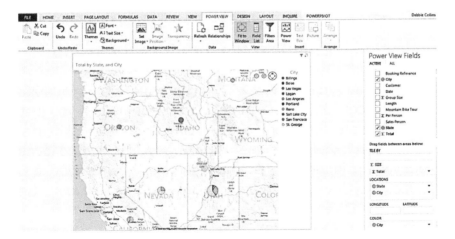

14. Re-enable the checkbox, **City**. The report is now reconfigured so the Total sales in some States are represented by a Pie Chart containing a breakdown of the sales within multiple Cities.

15. Hover over some of the pie slices to see the details. Double-click a State pie chart to drill down and display the Power View report by City (if the pie charts don't drill down, make sure you dragged both State and City into the Locations field in the Power View Fields).

16. In the upper-right corner of the map, to the left of the **Show Filters** and **Pop In** icons, is the **Drill Up** icon. Click the **Drill Up** icon to return back to the parent view.

Inquire Add-in

Another Excel add-in, included with Office Professional Plus 2013, is the new "Inquire" tool. This tool is useful when working with multiple workbooks or multiple worksheets. Once enabled, this tool can help you analyze workbooks for data dependencies, formula errors, hidden information, and broken links. It can diagram relationships between cells, worksheets and workbooks, compare between two versions of a workbook, and it has a Clean Excess Cell Formatting button. A new tab is created on the Ribbon when the Inquire add-in is enabled.

The Inquire Add-in is included only in the Office Professional Plus 2013 edition. Some readers of this book won't have Office Professional Plus 2013, so won't be able to participate in the following demonstration.

Demonstration – Enabling the Inquire Add-in Tab

1. The Inquire add-in is available in Office Professional Plus 2013. It is built-into Excel 2013, you simply need to enable it. If you just completed a previous demonstration in this chapter, skip this step. Otherwise, in Excel 2013 select **File>Open**. Select the location where you unzipped the demonstration files downloaded in Chapter One (i.e., SkyDrive or Computer). **Browse** to *Sales.xlsx*. Select it and click the **Open** button.

2. On the *Sales.xlsx* workbook, select the **Tours Booked** tab.

3. Select the **File** tab, select **Options**, and select **Add-Ins**.

4. At the bottom, in the **Manage** box, use the drop-down menu to change the selection to **COM Add-ins**. Click the **Go** button.

5. Check the box for **Inquire**, and then click **OK**.

6. The Ribbon should now have the **Inquire** tab.

Chapter Summary

This chapter examined the new features of Excel 2013 using a hands-on approach. New features supporting collaboration were: Sharing on SkyDrive, Get a Sharing Link and Post to Social Networks.

Excel 2013 has forty-eight new functions that were not available in previous versions, plus two functions that were moved to another category, and two functions that were renamed. These functions are listed on the Formulas tab in the Function Library under the following categories: Date & Time, Engineering, Financial, Information, Logical, Lookup & Reference, Math & Trig, Statistical, Text and Web.

Flash Fill was introduced as one of the most time-saving features of Excel 2013. When you enter data into a new column, if a pattern is recognized from adjacent columns, Excel automatically completes the remaining entries for you. Flash Fill can extract or concatenate data, reverse last and first names, insert letters or symbols or numbers, and speed up many other tasks which were complex and tedious in earlier versions of Excel.

The new Quick Analysis Tool was discussed and explored. It provides convenient live previews of the five most common analysis actions performed on data - Formatting, Charts, Totals, Tables and Sparklines.

Several improvements designed to make advanced charting and tables friendlier to mainstream users were examined - Recommended Charts, Chart Formatting Control, Chart Animation, Recommended PivotTables, and Timeline Filters.

You learned how to modify a data model using PowerPivot and how to create an interactive map using an advanced reporting feature called, Power View. Both are features included in only Office Professional Plus 2013.

Finally, this chapter demonstrated how to enable the Inquire add-in, which is an advanced tool used to analyze multiple workbooks and worksheets for dependencies and errors.

Chapter 5:
New Features of
PowerPoint 2013

This chapter covers the following topics:

- ✓ Theme Variants
- ✓ Eyedropper
- ✓ Co-editing
- ✓ Online Media
- ✓ Alignment Guides
- ✓ Merge Shapes
- ✓ Presenter View

Few new features were added to PowerPoint 2013. Instead, Microsoft has focused on helping users get the most out of the features that already existed in PowerPoint 2007 and PowerPoint 2010.

In this chapter, we will examine the new templates and themes available when you build a presentation. Collaboration similarities will be compared between Word 2013 and PowerPoint 2013. Next, we will explore several new features designed to make familiar tasks faster and easier to perform. Those features are inserting Online Pictures and Online Video, the new Alignment Guides, and the ability to Merge Shapes. Last of all, we will look at some enhancements to Presenter View.

To master the new features presented in this chapter, you are encouraged to follow along with the hands-on demonstrations. You may use or create your own files; however, specific files are referenced in the instructions to help you master these features more quickly. Refer to Chapter One in this book for instructions on how to download the demonstration files.

Theme Variants

Launch PowerPoint 2013 and the first thing you'll notice is that your choice of templates changed – the templates are wider! The new default templates have an aspect ratio of 16:9 to accommodate the screens of today's computing devices. Of course, the legacy 4:3 templates are still available to you. Once you choose a template, the next option allows you to change the color-scheme and other theme variants. Let's explore…

Demonstration – The New PowerPoint Templates

1. Launch PowerPoint 2013.

2. When PowerPoint 2013 opens the first time, or if you select **New**, several templates appear. Notice they all have the new 16:9 aspect ratio. These are the templates available to you while offline.

3. There are many more templates on Office.com. To view these templates you must be connected to the Internet. Under the Search box, select the **Business** category on the menu bar and you will see the themed templates located on Office.com. You can also view these templates organized in more refined categories using the pane on the far right.

4. On the menu bar across the top, to the left of the Search box, click the **Home** icon to return to the default templates.

5. Choose the template, **Ion**.

6. When you select **Ion**, that template will be displayed in the center of your screen and you will be provided the option to change the color scheme. At the bottom of the **Ion** slide are **left and right arrows** that allow you to navigate through slide layouts in the **Ion** template. Change the color scheme a few times to see the changes then scroll through the slides to see the effect.

7. When finished, click **X** the in upper-right corner to close the template.

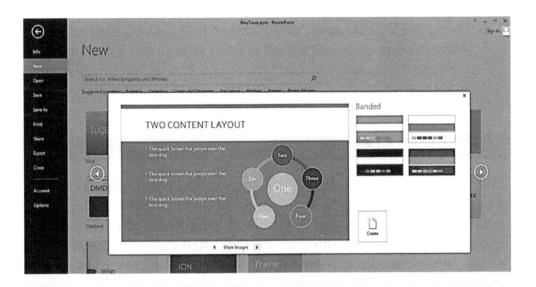

Eyedropper

Have you ever faced the challenge of making colors in your presentation match a company logo or colors in a photo? Microsoft has added a new tool to overcome this challenge. To precisely control color, the **Drawing Tools** tab now includes an "Eyedropper" under four of the fill buttons. The **Eyedropper** tool allows you to sample a color in a photo or logo in your presentation and apply that exact color to text and shapes elsewhere in your presentation. Color consistency is now easy to control with this tool.

Demonstration – Using the Eyedropper

1. In PowerPoint 2013 select **File>Open**. Select the location where you unzipped the demonstration files you downloaded in Chapter One (i.e., SkyDrive or Computer). **Browse** to *BikeTours.pptx*. Select it and click the **Open** button.

2. On the last slide (slide 8), select only the text inside the text box, "Any other suggestions?"

3. Select the Drawing Tools **Format** tab. In the **WordArt Styles** group, open the **Text Fill** drop-down menu and select the **Eyedropper.**

   Note: The **Eyedropper** tool is available under **Text Fill**, **Text Outline**, **Shape Fill** and **Shape Outline**.

4. Using the **Eyedropper**, select the red color filling the text, **Advertising**. A color box will appear next to the Eyedropper to indicate the color selected. When you can verify the color selected is **Dark Red**, click. The color of the text "Any other suggestions?" should change to match the **Dark Red**.

Co-editing

The same steps used to share documents and collaborate in Word 2013 and Excel 2013 also apply to PowerPoint 2013. When saving a PowerPoint presentation to SkyDrive or SharePoint, the owner can choose who to share it with and whether each invitee can view or edit the slides. After the editing permissions are setup, the owner can send the invitees an access link via email. The greatest advantage of collaborating within the cloud is that your invitees are assured they are seeing the latest version of your slides. PowerPoint 2013 also integrates with social networking sites by allowing you to embed a SkyDrive link on a blog or social network page that lets others view or edit your document.

Users of a business or professional edition of PowerPoint 2013 can take collaboration to a higher level with Lync. A PowerPoint author can opt to collaborate with others via a Lync conversation or meeting. With Lync, the author can grant other participants in the meeting live control of the presentation.

This section examines two enhancements that support co-editing in PowerPoint 2013: **Share** and **Reply to Comment**.

Share

Sharing PowerPoint 2013 slides on SkyDrive was introduced in Office 2010, but in Office 2013 it's simpler. Similar to other Office 2013 applications, under the **File** tab in the **Backstage** view of PowerPoint 2013 is a new feature called, **Share**. This feature replaces Save & Send, which was in Office 2010. All of the options that were in Save & Send still exist in **Share**, and a few new ones have been added. The process for sharing in PowerPoint 2013 is very similar to sharing in Word 2013 and Excel 2013.

Demonstration – Sharing Slides on SkyDrive

1. If you just completed the previous demonstration in this chapter, skip this step. Otherwise, in PowerPoint 2013 select **File>Open**. Select the location where you unzipped the demonstration files downloaded in Chapter One (i.e., SkyDrive or Computer). **Browse** to the file *BikeTours.pptx*. Select it and click the **Open** button.

2. Select **File>Share**. Four options will display: **Invite People, Email, Present Online,** and **Publish Slides**. Email and Publish Slides are the same as they were in PowerPoint 2010 under Save & Send. Present Online is simply a name change from Broadcast Slide Show in PowerPoint 2010. For this demonstration, select **Invite People**.

3. When **Invite People** is selected, a button will be displayed in the right pane called, **Save to Cloud**. Click it. This will actually take you to **File>Save As**. Three options are displayed under **Save As** which are: **SkyDrive**, **Computer** (i.e., local drive or network drive) and **Add a Place** (i.e., Office 365 SharePoint).

   Note: A fourth option will display if you are signed into an Office 365 account, **Other Web Locations** (i.e., SharePoint or another online storage service).

4. Select **SkyDrive**. If you completed either of the collaboration demonstrations in Chapter Three or Four, you will see a **Browse** button in the right pane. If you see **Browse**, skip to step 7.

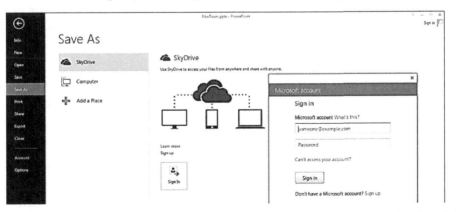

5. If instead of a **Browse** button you see a **Sign In** button in the right pane, click it and provide the credentials you created when you setup your SkyDrive account in Chapter Two. This connects Office

2013 to your SkyDrive. If you did not create a SkyDrive account in Chapter Two, click the Sign up link and create an account first, then click **Sign In**.

6. When PowerPoint 2013 is connected to your SkyDrive, its name will be displayed and you will be provided a button to **Browse** it.

   Note: If you later want to disconnect PowerPoint 2013 from an online service, such as SkyDrive, go to the **File>Account** option. Below your photo, click **Sign Out**. Or, for other connections, choose the **Connected Service** from the list and click the **Remove** link. To reconnect to SkyDrive, repeat steps 3 thru 6 above.

7. Click the **Browse** button. This will open your SkyDrive.

8. Browse to the folder you created in Chapter Three that you named, *Office 2013 Book Demos*. If you did not create this folder in Chapter Three, create it now by clicking **New Folder.** Save *BikeTours.pptx* into this SkyDrive folder.

9. After you save your file to SkyDrive, PowerPoint 2013 will automatically return you to **Invite People**. In the top field, enter the email addresses of people with whom you want to share your file. You can validate the email addresses by clicking the first icon to the right of the name field. You can also choose names from your Outlook Address Book by clicking the second icon to the right of the name field.

10. The drop-down menu to the right of the name field allows you to choose the file access you are granting this specific list of people: **Can view** or **Can edit.**

11. You can also include a message in your invitation by typing it into the message field.

12. When you have finished configuring your invitation, click the **Share** button. SkyDrive may prompt you for additional information. If so, click the link for additional authentication and follow the instructions. An email will automatically be sent to your invitees that includes your message and link to your file. Your list of invitees will also display under **Shared With** so you'll always know who can access this file.

Get a Sharing Link and Post to Social Networks

Permission to view or edit files on SkyDrive is embedded in the access link provided to a viewer. Once a file has been placed onto SkyDrive, you share it by sending others either a link to view, or a link to edit.

If you want your invitees to be identified on the document's **Share** pane, use **Invite People** to generate the access links. If listing each individual's identity on the **Share** pane is not important and you'd rather have the convenience of inviting people by group, you can **Get a Sharing Link** and send it in a bulk email. Another way to share with groups of people is to embed a link onto a web page, blog, or post it on a social networking site.

Demonstration – Generating a Sharing Link

1. This demonstration requires that you complete the previous **Demonstration – Sharing Slides on SkyDrive**. After a file is saved on SkyDrive, two new options will appear under **File>Share**: **Get a Sharing Link** (or **Get a Link**) and **Post to Social Networks**. Select **Get a Sharing Link** (or **Get a Link).**

2. In the right pane are two fields: **View Link** and **Edit Link**. To the right of each of these empty fields is a button, **Create Link**. Click each of these buttons to generate the two types of links.

3. After generating the type of link you want, simply copy the link and paste it into a group email or onto a web page. Anyone who clicks the link will be taken to your file and have the level of access specified by the link. At the bottom of the pane, under **Shared With,** the links are listed to remind you of their existence for this file.

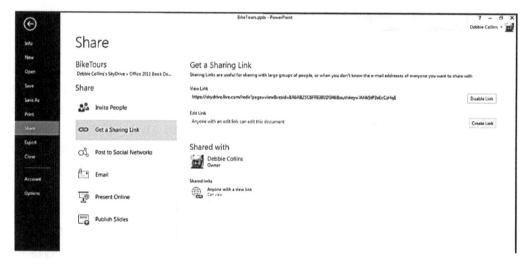

4. To test your links, copy the **View Link** you generated and paste it into your browser. This opens the file on SkyDrive. Notice you can **Download**, **Print**, **Start Slide Show** or make **Comments**, but you cannot **Share** the file, nor edit anything. You have View access only.

5. Next, copy the **Edit Link** and paste it into your browser. Just like with View permission, you can **Download** and **Print** the file, you can **Start Slide Show** or see and make **Comments**, but you cannot

Share the file; however, you now have the option to **Edit in Browser**. Click this menu tab to see how it works.

6. If prompted, **Sign in** by providing your SkyDrive credentials.

7. Once signed in, when a user clicks **Edit Presentation** two options are provided: **Edit in PowerPoint** and **Edit in PowerPoint Web App**. Either option allows the user to make changes to the slides.

8. When you've finished exploring shared editing of your file, in the upper-right corner click **Sign Out**. Switch back to PowerPoint 2013.

9. To revoke a link's access to your slides, click the **Disable Link** button. This permanently removes the link. Once disabled, it is gone! It will no longer work and you cannot restore it, but you can generate a new one. To conclude this demonstration, revoke both links by clicking each of the **Disable Link** buttons.

Note: You can generate similar links for users to access complete folders on your SkyDrive. This must be done from within SkyDrive. After logging into http://www.skydrive.com, simply check the box to select the file or folder you want to share, then from the menu across the top of the screen select either **Share>Get a Link** or select **Embed.**

Demonstration – Posting Slides to Facebook

1. This demonstration requires that you completed the previous **Demonstration – Sharing Slides on SkyDrive**. You must also have a Facebook account. When you are connected to a PowerPoint file on SkyDrive, two new options will appear under **File>Share**: **Get a Sharing Link** (or **Get a Link**) and **Post to Social Networks**. Select **Post to Social Networks**.

2. What you now see in the right pane depends on what you selected when you setup your online Microsoft Account. Connectors to the following social networks are currently available for Office 2013: **Facebook, Twitter, LinkedIn, Flickr,** and **Google**. If your Microsoft account is connected to one or more of these networks, their icons appear in the right pane with a checkbox next to each icon. If **Facebook** is in the right pane, skip to step 10.

3. If you are not yet connected to any social networks, press the link **Click here to connect social networks** and then skip to step 5.

4. If one or more social networks appear in the right pane, but not Facebook. Go to the upper-right corner of the screen and click your name to open the drop-down menu. Click **About Me**. If prompted, **Sign in** to your Microsoft Account using your SkyDrive credentials. Under your name and photo, click **Connect** to open your online Microsoft Account.

5. The **Add Accounts** page will list the social networks that have not yet been added, but are available to your Microsoft Account. Click **Facebook**.

6. On the next page, click **Connect**. Login to your Facebook account.

7. On the Facebook **Request for Permission** page, click **Allow**. On the next page, click **Done**.

8. In the upper-right corner, click your name and **Sign out**.

9. Switch back to PowerPoint 2013, select **Post to Social Networks**. In the right pane, click the **Refresh** button. The Facebook logo should appear in the right pane.

10. Enable the checkbox next to the **Facebook** logo. Select the permission level to grant to your file: **Can View** or **Can Edit**.

11. Type in the message field, *This is a test – View my Bike slides*.

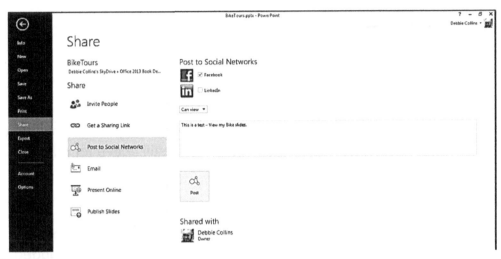

12. Click the **Post** button.

13. Go to **http://www.facebook.com** and login to your account.

14. Your post should appear on your Facebook wall. Click on the **Bike** link to test it. Just as in the **Demonstration – Generating a Sharing Link**, if the permission you set in step 10 was **Can View**, you should be able to **Download** and **Print** the file, **Start Slide Show** or see and make **Comments**, but you cannot **Share** the file, nor edit anything. You have View access only. If the permission you set in step 10 was **Can Edit**, you can also **Edit in Browser**.

15. When you're finished testing your link, return to PowerPoint 2013, **File>Share>Post to Social Networks**. In the right pane, under **Shared With**, right-click the Facebook icon. Select **Disable Posted Link.** It will be removed from PowerPoint 2013.

16. Return to your Facebook wall. Hover in the upper-right corner of your post to reveal the option to **Edit or Delete**. Click it. Select **Delete...** In the next dialog box click **Delete**.

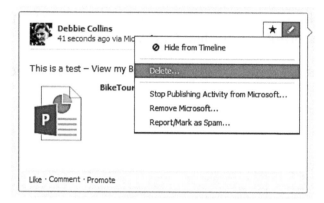

17. Your post on Facebook should be removed, but your connection between Office 2013 and Facebook is still active for other demonstrations in this book.

Reply to Comment

Just as in Word 2013, comments in PowerPoint 2013 now provide more powerful collaboration capabilities. A **Reply** field has been added below the original **Comment** which allows reviewers to comment about comments! The owner of each comment is identified by name and, if available, a photo. Hover over the photo and the commenter's **Contact Card** is displayed. Click the arrow in the lower right to **Open Contact Card** and display the commenter's address, phone number, email address and other information pulled from the commenter's SkyDrive profile.

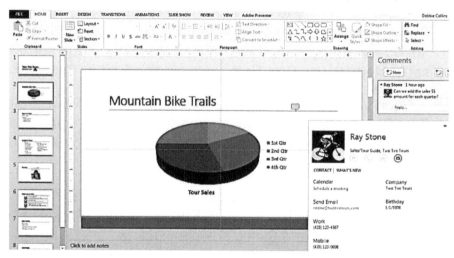

From the commenter's **Contact Card** you can click icons to communicate by **Instant Messenger**, **Voice**, **Video**, or **Email**. You can even click a link to schedule a meeting with the commenter using Outlook 2013!

Unlike Word 2013, there is not yet a Mark Comment Done option in PowerPoint 2013. Hopefully, Microsoft will add that option in the future.

Demonstration – Reply to Comment

1. If you just completed a previous demonstration in this chapter, skip this step. Otherwise, in PowerPoint 2013 select **File>Open**. Select the location where you unzipped the demonstration files downloaded in Chapter One (i.e., SkyDrive or Computer). **Browse** to the file *BikeTours.pptx*. Select it and click the **Open** button.

2. Go to **Slide 2**. Select the **Review** tab. In the **Comments** group, click **Show Comments** and select the option **Comments Pane**.

3. A comment from Ray Stone will appear on the right in the **Comments Pane**. Click the expansion arrow next to Ray Stone's name to open the comment. This will reveal a **Reply** field.

4. Type a reply to this comment, "I agree with Ray."

5. Hover over the photo in Ray's comment balloon to display Ray's **Contact Card**.

   Note: If you don't see a bicycle as Ray's photo, you must **Sign In** to your SkyDrive account. Unless you are connected to SkyDrive, you will not see any information in the commenters **Contact Card**. Go to the upper-right corner of PowerPoint and click **Sign In**. Click the default option, **Microsoft Account**. Enter your credentials and click the **Sign In** button.

6. In the lower right corner of Ray's Contact Card, click the arrow icon **Open Contact Card**. Notice the four contact icons just below Ray's title. They are **Instant Messenger, Phone**, **Video,** and **Email**. Also, under the **Calendar**, notice the link to schedule a meeting.

Online Media

Three new media options appear on the Insert tab. The first is a new button called **Online Pictures**. **Online Pictures** replaces the Clip Art button of Office 2007 and Office 2010. Two other options have changed names: Video from Web Site... has been renamed **Online Video...,** and Clip Art Audio... has been renamed **Online Audio...** Both of these options are located in the **Media** group under the **Video** and **Audio** buttons. These features allow you to insert media from Office.com or any source on the Internet. PowerPoint 2013 can access images from Office.com, Bing, and other services. This improvement allows you to add images to a slide from the Web without having to save them first to your desktop.

PowerPoint 2013 now supports .mp4, .m4v, and .mov video formats in addition to the .asf, .avi, .mpg (.mpeg), .swf and .wmv formats supported in PowerPoint 2010. Likewise, .m4a and .mp4 audio formats are now supported in PowerPoint 2013 in addition to the legacy .aiff, .au, .mid (.midi), .mp3, .wav and .wma audio formats supported in earlier versions. So, you no longer need to convert these popular video and audio formats before using them in your PowerPoint 2013 presentation. In fact, for the best playback experience Microsoft recommends using .mp4 videos encoded with H.264 video (a.k.a. MPEG-4 AVC) and AAC audio.

Demonstration – Inserting Online Pictures and Video

1. If you just completed a previous demonstration in this chapter, skip this step. Otherwise, in PowerPoint 2013 select **File>Open**. Select the location where you unzipped the demonstration files downloaded in Chapter One (i.e., SkyDrive or Computer). **Browse** to the file *BikeTours.pptx*. Select it and click the **Open** button.

2. Go to **Slide 5**. Under the title **Scenery**, delete the photo.

3. On the **Insert** tab, in the **Images** group, click **Online Pictures**. In the **Office.com Clip Art** field enter, *Mountain Biker*.

4. Choose a photo and click **Insert**.

5. Above the Ribbon, on the **Quick Access Toolbar**, click the **Undo** button to delete the picture.

6. On the **Insert** tab, in the **Media** group, click **Video** and select **Online Video**. In the **Bing Video Search** field enter, *Slickrock Trail*. Choose a video and click **Insert**.

7. To test your video playback, do the following: Select the video. Select the **Video Tools Playback** tab. In the **Video Options** group, click the drop-down menu next to **Start:** and select either **Automatically** or **On Click**. Select the **Slideshow** tab and click **From Current Slide**.

8. When finished, leave the video in place for the next demonstration.

Alignment Guides

Guides exist in previous versions of PowerPoint; however, they now have enhanced capabilities. Guides can now be placed in a unique location on each Slide Master Layout, so they are displayed in that exact same location on every slide using that layout.

When you enable the original Guides, another set of guides are also enabled in PowerPoint 2013 called, "Alignment Guides". These new **Alignment Guides** operate the same as in Word 2013. Simply drag a chart, image, shape, video, or SmartArt towards the edge or center of the slide, and an **Alignment Guide** automatically appears to mark the vertical center, or margins on the slide. These special **Alignment Guides** appear only when you need them and disappear when you're done.

Demonstration – Using Alignment Guides

1. Complete **Demonstration – Inserting Online Pictures and Video** prior to attempting this demonstration.

2. Select the video you inserted in the previous demonstration. Drag it to the center of the slide and up towards the upper margin. Notice the subtle dashed Alignment Guides marking the center of the slide and the top margin.

3. Drag the video around on the document and notice Alignment Guides appear and disappear marking the left margin, right margin, top and bottom margins, and center of the slide.

4. When finished exploring the Alignment Guides, drag the video to the center of the slide and leave it for the next demonstration.

Merge Shapes

A convenient new feature in PowerPoint 2013 is the capability to create new shapes by merging existing shapes. On the **Format** tab of the **Drawing Tools**, in the **Shapes** group, is a new **Merge Shapes** button. The options under this new button are **Union**, **Combine**, **Fragment**, **Intersect**, and **Subtract**. Building shapes directly in PowerPoint 2013 is much more convenient than building shapes in Visio and copying them to PowerPoint.

Demonstration – Merging Shapes

1. If you just completed a previous demonstration in this chapter, skip this step. Otherwise, in PowerPoint 2013 select **File>Open**. Select the location where you unzipped the demonstration files downloaded in Chapter One (i.e., SkyDrive or Computer). **Browse** to the file *BikeTours.pptx*. Select it and click the **Open** button.

2. Go to **Slide 5**. On the **View** tab check the box to enable **Guides**.

3. On the **Insert** tab, in the **Illustrations** group, click the **Shapes** button. Under **Block Arrows**, select **Right Arrow**. Under the title **Scenery**, below the image, draw the right arrow so it occupies the space from the center guide to the right edge of the image.

4. Repeat the step above to create a **Left Arrow** butted up against the right arrow in the center and pointing in the opposite direction to the left edge of the image.

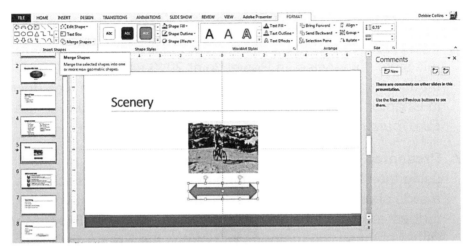

5. Select both arrow images. On the **Drawing Tools Format** tab, in the **Insert Shapes** group, click **Merge Shapes** and select **Union**.

6. The two shapes should now be joined into one shape that you can move it around the slide as a single object.

Presenter View

Presenting in PowerPoint 2013 is much easier than previous versions. "Presenter View" has new features to help you to stay organized, jump around in your slides while answering questions, and better engage your audience. The new features include:

- **Auto-extend** - When projecting to a screen, this setting ensures that your speaker notes and navigation tools are displayed on the monitor that only you can see.

- **Navigation Grid** - This new feature allows you to visually jump around in a presentation without the audience's awareness. From the grid, you can show slides in and out of sequence. The Navigation Grid is especially useful when answering questions at the end of a presentation.

- **Slide Zoom** – In PowerPoint 2013, you can direct your audience's attention by zooming in on a diagram, chart, or graphic with a couple of clicks. This is useful for displaying details during a discussion.

Demonstration – Using Presenter View

1. If you just completed a previous demonstration in this chapter, skip this step. Otherwise, in PowerPoint 2013 select **File>Open**. Select the location where you unzipped the demonstration files downloaded in Chapter One (i.e., SkyDrive or Computer). **Browse** to the file *BikeTours.pptx*. Select it and click the **Open** button.

2. **Presenter View** can be accessed two different ways. The first is by using the short-cut key combination **ALT+F5**. The second is to start a slide show and use the icons in the lower-left corner. Click the furthest icon from the left margin and select **Show Presenter View**. Either of these two methods will launch the **Presenter View**.

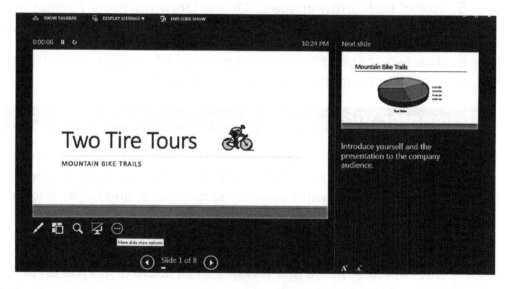

3. In **Presenter View**, the slide projected to the audience is displayed on the left. The next slide to be next is displayed on the right. The speaker's notes are displayed below it. Across the bottom of the current slide are icons. The "Navigation Grid" is accessed using the second icon from the left labeled **Show All Slides**. Click it and explore how to jump around your slides using the Navigation Grid.

4. Click the icon that looks like a magnifying glass, **Zoom into the Slide**. Move the zoom box over the portion of the slide you'd like to enlarge, and then click. You can use the Hand to pan the enlarged area around the slide. When finished, click the **Zoom** icon again, or press the **ESC** key.

5. If you never used **Presenter View** in previous versions of PowerPoint, take a few moments to explore it now. When finished, click the last icon **More Slide Show Options** and select **End Show**, or press the **ESC** key.

Chapter Summary

This chapter examined the new features of PowerPoint 2013 using a hands-on approach. New templates were introduced that have an aspect ratio of 16:9. Many of these templates allow you to change the color scheme. The new Eyedropper tool helps control color consistency by sampling a color and applying that color to text or shapes elsewhere in the presentation.

New features supporting collaboration were explored, such as Sharing on SkyDrive, Get a Sharing Link and Post to Social Networks. You experienced how permissions can be granted to others using links.

New media options were examined on the Insert tab. Online Pictures replaced the Clip Art button of Office 2007 and Office 2010. Two other options changed names: Video from Web Site... was renamed Online Video..., Clip Art Audio... was renamed Online Audio...

Alignment Guides appear when new objects are dragged around the page. Alignment Guides mark the margins and the center of the slide to help position items more accurately.

Merge Shapes creates new shapes from existing shapes using four options: Union, Combine, Fragment, Intersect, and Subtract.

Finally, this chapter examined a few enhancements made to Presenter View: the Navigation Grid and Slide Zoom.

Chapter 6:
New Features of
OneNote 2013

This chapter covers the following topics:

✓   Improved Search
✓   Co-editing
✓   Support for Mobile and Touch Devices
✓   Converting Handwritten Notes to Type
✓   Embedded Files
✓   Enhanced Tables
✓   Send to OneNote Utility

OneNote is now included in all editions of Office 2013, except Mac. However, since there is also a OneNote Web App, anyone with a web browser, including Mac users, can benefit from this program. OneNote is linked to the other Office 2013 applications, so it's easy to move information back-and-forth. It is by far the best auxiliary application on the planet for gathering notes, links, webpages, sketches, and media into a single collection of usable information. In fact, OneNote was used to collect the researched content for this book!

OneNote 2013 is not much different than OneNote 2010, except it has been optimized to run on either Windows 7 or Windows 8. If run on Windows 8, OneNote 2013 inherits the Metro look and touch capabilities.

In this chapter, we will examine the faster search capability of OneNote 2013. Collaboration similarities will be compared with Word 2013 and PowerPoint 2013 and we'll play with the new bookmarking feature in Reading Resume.   Next, we will examine how mobile and touch devices are supported by OneNote 2013. Handwriting conversion to type will be discussed. Support for embedded files will be explored. Last of all, we will look at improvements for working with tables and how to use the new Send to OneNote taskbar utility.

To master the new features presented in this chapter, you are encouraged to follow along with the hands-on demonstrations. You may use or create your own files; however, specific files are referenced in the instructions to help you master these features more quickly. Refer to Chapter One in this book for instructions on how to download the demonstration files.

Improved Search

Searching is faster and more accurate in OneNote 2013,. As in previous versions, you can search for terms in a note, link, or title of a file. But, most impressive is OneNote's capability to search for text in pictures! This feature existed in OneNote 2010, but now it's so fast that it is almost instantaneous! Basically, in OneNote 2013 you can search for just about any term you've captured. Let's experience how it works....

Demonstration – Searching Text in Photos

1. In OneNote 2013, select **File>Open**. Select the location where you unzipped the demonstration files you downloaded in Chapter One (i.e., SkyDrive or Computer). At the bottom of the browse window, change the file extension in the drop-down menu to display files that are formatted as a **OneNote Single File Package (*.onepkg)**. Select *TwoTireTours.onepkg*. Click the **Open** button.

2. When prompted to **Specify the Notebook Properties**, keep the **Name:** *TwoTireTours*. Accept the default color. Change the **Path:** to the location where you opened the file. Click **Create**.

3. On the far right in the **Search** field, you are going to type a term. Begin by typing just the first letter *D*. Notice the list of results displayed in the pane below and the first occurrence is highlighted in yellow on the first page of notes. The result is instantaneous!

4. Now, keep typing the rest of the search term, *Delicate Arch*. As you type, the list of results will get shorter until only **Photos** remains.

5. Click on the **Photos** result and you will be taken to the **Photo Album** section tab. Notice the text in the **Delicate Arch** photo is highlighted to match the search term.

6. All photos that have text are searchable by default. If you want to disable this feature, right-click the photo. At the bottom of the menu, select **Make Text in Image Searchable…**, click **Disabled.**

Co-editing

Although you can choose to save your notes to any location, OneNote 2013 prefers to be saved to SkyDrive or SharePoint by default. This makes backups, mobile access, and sharing with others easy.

You can share pages, sections, or notebooks in OneNote. The process is similar to sharing other Office 2013 files, but a little different. Just as with the other Office 2013 applications, you first save the OneNote file on SkyDrive or SharePoint, then send your friends a link to the file with permissions to view or edit. Once the notes are stored online, you can be assured that everyone is accessing the latest version. Storing online also assures that you can access your notes from all your mobile devices.

As in previous versions of OneNote, your notes are automatically saved so you can't forget.

Users of a business or professional edition of OneNote 2013 will discover it is the default application for meeting notes during a Lync connection. Lync automatically captures a list of meeting participants into OneNote. Note taking is initiated from the Meeting tab within Outlook. More about this feature is discussed in Chapter 7, New Features in Outlook 2013.

Share

The option to Share in OneNote 2013 is located under the **File** tab in the **Backstage** view, similar to other Office 2013 applications. The **Share** option existed in OneNote 2010, but in OneNote 2013 it's been redesigned to be more consistent with the other Office 2013 applications.

Demonstration – Sharing a Notebook on SkyDrive

1. If you just completed the previous demonstration, skip this step. Otherwise in OneNote 2013, select **File>Open**. Select the location where you unzipped the demonstration files you downloaded in Chapter One (i.e., SkyDrive or Computer). At the bottom of the browse window, change the file extension in the drop-down menu to display files that are formatted as a **OneNote Single File Package (*.onepkg)**. Select *TwoTireTours.onepkg*. Click the **Open** button. When prompted to Specify the Notebook Properties, keep the **Name:** *TwoTireTours*. Accept the default color. Change the **Path:** to the location where you opened the file. Click **Create**.

2. Select **File>Share**. In OneNote 2013, Share looks more like Save As in the other Office 2013 applications. Two options display: **SkyDrive** and **Add a Place** (i.e., Office 365 SharePoint or another SkyDrive). Select **SkyDrive**. If you completed the collaboration demonstration in either Chapter Three, Four, or Five, you will see a **Move Notebook** button in the right pane. If you see **Move Notebook**, skip to step 4

   Note: A third option will display if you are signed into an Office 365 account, **Other Web Locations** (i.e., SharePoint or another online storage service).

3. If instead of a **Browse** button you see a **Sign In** button in the right pane, click it and provide the credentials you created when you setup your SkyDrive account in Chapter Two. This connects Office 2013 to your SkyDrive. If you did not create a SkyDrive account in Chapter Two, click the Sign up link instead and create an account first, then click **Sign In**.

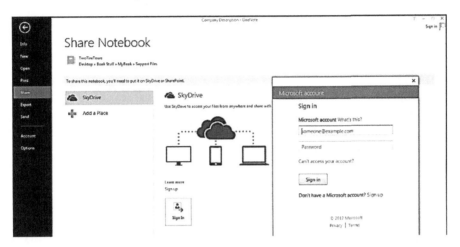

4. OneNote 2013 will recognize the name of your notebook as **TwoTireTours**. Accept this default. Click **Move Notebook** to save the notebook to the cloud in preparation for sharing.

5. After your notebook is synchronized to SkyDrive, you will receive a confirmation. Click **OK**.

6. After your notebook is saved on SkyDrive, Share will display four options: **Invite People**, **Get a Sharing Link (Get a Link)**, **Share with Meeting**, and **Move Notebook**. Select **Invite People**. We will explore the other options later.

7. To invite people to view or edit your OneNote 2013 file simply enter their email addresses into the field. You can validate the email addresses by clicking the first icon to the right of the name field. You can also choose names from your Outlook Address Book by clicking the second icon to the right of the name field.

8. The drop-down menu to the right of the name field allows you to choose the file access you are granting this specific list of people: **Can view** or **Can edit.**

9. You can also include a message in your invitation by typing it into the message field.

10. When you have finished configuring your invitation, click the **Share** button. SkyDrive may prompt you for additional information. If so, click the link for additional authentication and follow the instructions. An email will automatically be sent to your invitees that includes your message and link to your file. Your list of invitees will also display under **Shared With** so you'll always know who can access this file.

Get a Sharing Link

Permission to view or edit files on SkyDrive is embedded in the access link provided to a viewer. Once a file has been placed onto SkyDrive, you share it by sending others either a link to view, or a link to edit.

If you want your invitees to be identified on the document's **Share** pane, use **Invite People** to generate the access links. If listing each individual's identity on the **Share** pane is not important and you'd rather have the convenience of inviting people by group, you can **Get a Sharing Link** and send it in a bulk email.

Demonstration – Generating a Sharing Link

1. This demonstration requires that you complete the previous
   Demonstration – Sharing a Notebook on SkyDrive. After your
   notebook is saved on SkyDrive, several options will appear under
   File>Share. Select **Get a Sharing Link (or Get a Link)**

2. In the right pane are two fields: **View Link** and **Edit Link**. To the
   right of each of these empty fields is a button, **Create Link**. Click
   each of these buttons to generate the two types of links.

3. After generating the type of link you want, simply copy the link and
   paste it into a group email or onto a web page. Anyone who clicks
   the link will be taken to your document and have the level of access
   specified by the link. At the bottom of the pane, under **Shared With**,
   the links are listed to remind you of their existence for this file.

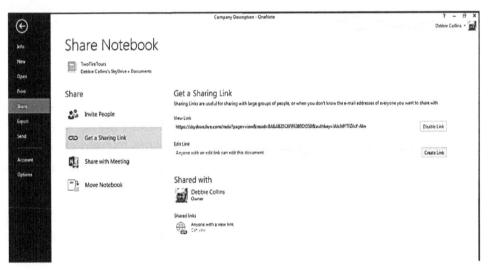

4. To test your links, copy the **View Link** you generated and paste it
   into your browser. This opens the notebook on SkyDrive. Notice
   you are limited to reading the notebook. You can also select items
   and right-click, **Copy**. You cannot **Share** the file, nor edit anything.
   Unlike some of the other Office 2013 applications, you cannot
   download or print. You have View access only.

5. Next, copy the **Edit Link** and paste it into your browser. Just like with View permission, you can read and copy, but you cannot **Share** the file; however, you now have the option to **Edit Notebook**. Click this menu tab to see how it works.

6. If prompted, **Sign in** by providing your SkyDrive credentials.

7. When a user clicks **Edit Notebook** two options are provided: **Edit in Microsoft OneNote** and **Edit in OneNote Web App**. Either option allows the user to make changes to the Notebook.

8. When you've finished exploring shared editing, in the upper-right corner click **Sign Out**. Switch back to OneNote 2013.

9. To revoke a link's access to your file, click the **Disable Link** button. This permanently removes the link. Once disabled, it is gone! It will no longer work and you cannot restore it, but you can generate a new one. To conclude this demonstration, revoke both links by clicking each of the **Disable Link** buttons.

Share Notes During Meetings

Online remote meetings are becoming more common in businesses today. But, why take notes on your own when OneNote can be shared and makes it possible for all the meeting participants to help? If everyone contributes to the note taking, you're less likely to miss an action item or a key point in the meeting discussion.

OneNote 2013 makes it easy to share notes during a Lync meeting. Unfortunately, this cannot be demonstrated without a meeting connection, but here are the basic steps:

1. Within OneNote, click anywhere on the page you want to share with the meeting participants. This selects the specific note page.

2. Go to **File>Share**. Select **Share with Meeting**.

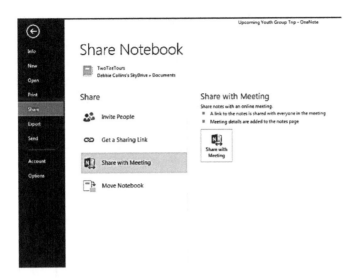

3. If you are connected to any meetings, they will appear in a pop-up. Select a meeting and a link to the page is sent to all participants.

Prepare Note Sharing Before Meetings

If you are responsible for setting up a meeting and you know in advance that you're going to share notes with the participants, you can create a shared OneNote page from Outlook 2013.

A meeting OneNote page is created automatically and a link to the page is sent to all the meeting participants in their Lync meeting invitation.

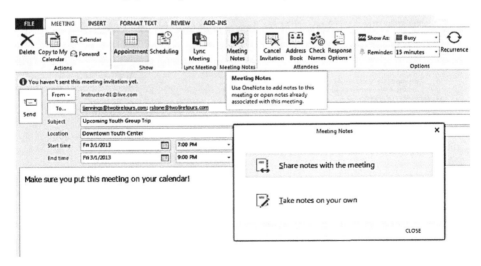

The OneNote page contains all the details about where the meeting was and who attended, so you and the participants can jump right into taking notes. A list of invited participants is included with checkboxes by each name so you can track their attendance. If you're the meeting organizer and you make a change to the location or time, your notes will get updated when you send the update from Outlook.

If you're not the organizer, you can right-click on the page tab and select **Refresh Meeting Details** to have it update.

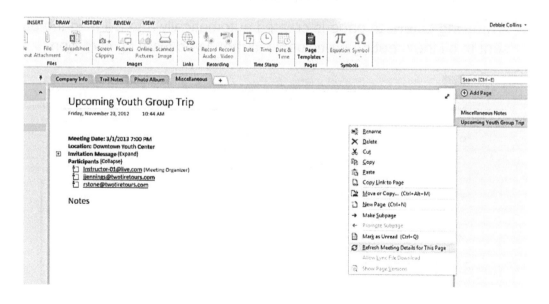

Support for Mobile and Touch Devices

OneNote has Mobile apps for all popular devices: Windows Phone, iOS devices, and Android phones. These can be downloaded from the app store for that device. If an app doesn't yet exist for your particular mobile device, no problem....simply use an Internet browser to open your SkyDrive where your notes are stored and use the OneNote Web App!

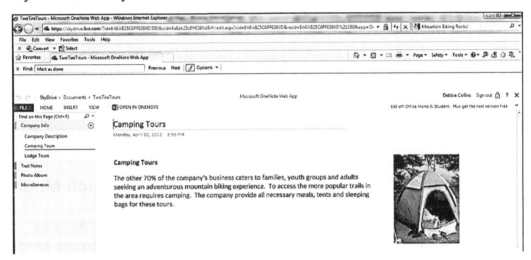

Bookmarking for Mobile Access

Resume Reading is a new feature integrated across all the Office 2013 applications. It works with syncing and cross-device support. Together, these technologies provide an automatic "bookmarking" capability that ensures you always resume reading a file where you exited. For example, if you exit your notebook using a PC at home and then later access the same notebook from work or school using a tablet or smartphone, you will resume exactly where you left off!

Demonstration – Reading Resume

1. This demonstration requires that you complete the previous **Demonstration – Sharing a Notebook on SkyDrive**. After your notebook is saved on SkyDrive, select the **Company Info** section tab in your **TwoTireTours** notebook.

2. In the **Company Info** section of your notebook, on the right side, select the **Camping Tours** page.

3. Exit OneNote by clicking the **X** in the upper-right corner.

4. Reopen OneNote 2013. It should automatically resume where you exited on the **Camping Tours** page.

Touch Mode

On touch capable devices, it is usually desirable to have more space between buttons and commands to accommodate control of OneNote with your fingers. On keyboard/mouse devices, it is usually desirable to have buttons and commands closer together to use screen space more efficiently. To change from Mouse Mode to Touch Mode, you must first enable the switcher on the Quick Access Toolbar at the top of the screen

Demonstration – Switching Mouse Mode to Touch Mode

1. In the upper-left corner of the screen, open the **Quick Access Toolbar**. At the bottom of the menu, enable **Touch/Mouse Mode.**

2. A drop-down menu will appear next to the **Quick Access Toolbar** that allows you to switch between **Mouse Mode** and **Touch Mode**. Choose either **Mouse Mode** or **Touch Mode**, whichever you desire to get the spacing you need between buttons.

Converting Handwritten Notes to Type

If you use OneNote 2013 on a touch capable device, you'll discover "inking" has been enhanced so you can draw and edit with a finger or stylus. If you'd rather write than type, handwriting conversion in OneNote 2013 converts writing to text more accurately than previous versions.

Handwriting notes is useful if you can write better or faster than you can type, and it's great for meetings where the sound of typing on a keyboard may be inappropriate.

This cannot be demonstrated without a touch capable device. If you have access to OneNote 2013 on a touch capable device, here are the basic steps to create handwritten notes and convert them to type.

1. On the OneNote 2013 Ribbon, click the **Draw** tab.

2. In the **Tools** group, click any of the color pens or highlighters, and then create some "handwritten notes" using your stylus or finger.

3. When you are finished creating your handwritten notes, on the **Draw** tab, click the **Type** button.

4. Drag to select the handwritten notes you want to convert.

5. On the **Draw** tab, in the **Convert** group, click **Ink to Text**.

Embedded Files

One of the most powerful uses of OneNote 2013 is its capability to insert pictures, documents, videos, and more into your notes. In OneNote 2013, if you insert an Excel spreadsheet or a Visio object, you can edit those embedded files inside OneNote 2013 using the original application that created them (i.e., Excel or Visio). This assumes, of course, that you also have Excel or Visio installed on the device that is editing the object in OneNote 2013.

Demonstration – Embed an Excel Table

1. If you just completed a previous demonstration, skip this step. Otherwise in OneNote 2013, select **File>Open**. Select the location where you unzipped the demonstration files you downloaded in Chapter One (i.e., SkyDrive or Computer). At the bottom of the browse window, change the file extension in the drop-down menu to display files that are formatted as a **OneNote Single File Package (*.onepkg)**. Select *TwoTireTours.onepkg*. Click the **Open** button. When prompted to **Specify the Notebook Properties**, keep the **Name:** *TwoTireTours*. Accept the default color. Change the **Path:** to the location where you opened the file. Click **Create**.

2. Select the **Miscellaneous** section tab. On the far right in the page navigation pane, select the **Miscellaneous Notes** page.

3. On the OneNote Ribbon, select the **Insert** tab. In the **Files** group, click **Spreadsheet** and select **Existing Excel Spreadsheet**.

4. Browse to the location where you unzipped the demonstration files you downloaded in Chapter One (i.e., SkyDrive or Computer). Select *Sales.xlsx* and click Insert. A window will open asking you to select one of three options for inserting the spreadsheet: **Attach File, Insert Spreadsheet** or **Insert a Chart or Table**.

5. Choose **Insert a Chart or Table.**

6. Another window will open allowing you to choose whether to insert the entire workbook (**Display Everything**), insert one or more worksheets (by name), or insert specific tables (by name). Choose to insert the table named **Winter Sales Qtr1_Summary**. Click **OK**.

7. The table from the Excel spreadsheet will be embedded onto the OneNote page.

8. If you want to change a value, click the **Edit** button just above the table. This button will open the table in Excel 2013 so that you have full editing capabilities. Change the value in cell H6 from $600.00 to $500.00. Save the file in Excel 2013 and notice the table embedded in OneNote 2013 is automatically updated. This does not change the original Excel 2013 file, only the table on the OneNote 2013 page. The advantage of using embedded files in OneNote 2013 is editing using the original application (i.e., Excel or Visio).

Enhanced Tables

Of course, you are not limited to only embedding tables into OneNote. You can also create them inside OneNote 2013. Table tools have been enhanced in OneNote 2013 to support simple formatting, making headers, rearranging rows and columns. If you'd like, you can convert a table in your notes into an embedded Excel spreadsheet with a single click!

Demonstration – Create and Format a Table

1. If you just completed a previous demonstration, skip this step. Otherwise in OneNote 2013, select **File>Open**. Select the location where you unzipped the demonstration files you downloaded in Chapter One (i.e., SkyDrive or Computer). At the bottom of the browse window, change the file extension in the drop-down menu to display files that are formatted as a **OneNote Single File Package (*.onepkg)**. Select *TwoTireTours.onepkg*. Click the **Open** button. When prompted to Specify the Notebook Properties, keep the **Name:** *TwoTireTours*. Accept the default color. Change the **Path:** to the location where you opened the file. Click **Create**.

2. Select the **Miscellaneous** section tab. On the far right in the page navigation pane, select **+ Add Page**. Name your new page, **Table**.

3. On the OneNote Ribbon, click the **Insert** tab. Click the Table button and create a table that is **5 columns** wide **by 4 rows** high. If you'd like, populate the cells with headings and data.

4. Notice a **Table Tools Layout** contextual tab appears with tools that allow you to format and modify a basic table. There are buttons that allow you to **Select, Insert** and **Delete** columns and rows, **Hide Borders**, and control **Alignment** - all of these existed in OneNote 2010. The buttons that are new to OneNote 2013 are **Shading, Sort**, and **Convert to Excel Spreadsheet.**

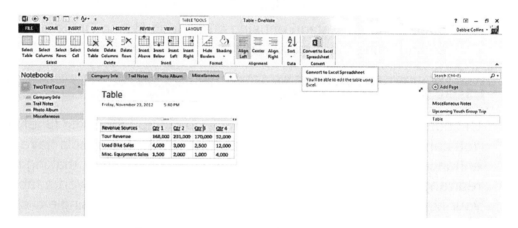

Send to OneNote Utility

A new utility included with OneNote 2013 is Send to OneNote. After you install OneNote 2013, this utility will reside on your taskbar. It allows you to send items to OneNote 2013 even when the application is not open.

Send to OneNote has three options. These options are described below:

- **Screen Clipping** – allows you to select a portion of a web page or document and "clip it" for saving into OneNote 2013. After you've made a selection, a dialog box will open allowing you to choose where to save it in OneNote 2013 (unless you've customized the Send to OneNote location under **File>Options>Send to OneNote**)

- **Send to OneNote** – an entire web page or printed document can be sent to OneNote 2013 with this option.   When you click this option, a dialog box will open allowing you to choose where to save the item in OneNote 2013 (unless you've customized the Send to OneNote location under **File>Options>Send to OneNote**)

- **New Quick Note** – pops open a small window so you can write a "quick note" that is saved into the unfiled Quick Notes section in the lower-left corner of OneNote 2013.

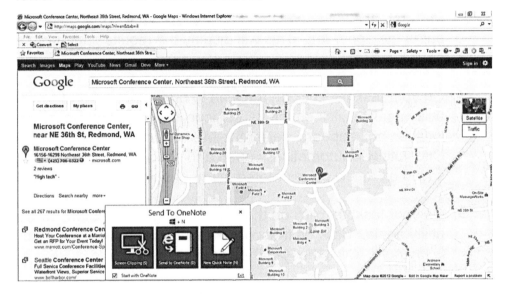

Demonstration – Send to OneNote

1. Close OneNote 2013 by clicking the **X** in the upper-right corner.

2. Using a browser, go to **http://www.google.com** and select **Maps** on the menu bar in the upper-left.

3. In the Search field type, *Microsoft Conference Center, Redmond.*

4. From your taskbar at the bottom of your computer screen, click on the icon to bring up the **Send to OneNote** utility. Click on **Screen Clipping**. Select the entire map.

5. A location box will appear (unless you've customized the Send to OneNote location). If necessary, expand the **TwoTireTours** notebook to see the sections. Select the **Miscellaneous** section in the **TwoTireTours** notebook. Click **OK**. OneNote 2013 will automatically open and you should see your map clipping saved on a new page.

6. Close OneNote 2013 by clicking the **X** in the upper-right corner.

7. Return to the web page used in step 2. Select **Search** on the menu bar in the upper-left. This will display the results page from your earlier search.

8. On your taskbar, click on the icon to bring up the **Send to OneNote** utility again. Click on the center icon, **Send to OneNote**. When the location box appears, select the **Miscellaneous** section. Click **OK**. OneNote will automatically open and you will see the search results saved on a new page created in the **Miscellaneous** section.

9. On your taskbar, click on the icon to bring up the **Send to OneNote** utility again. Click on the icon, **New Quick Note**. Type a note, *This is my note*. Click the **X** in the upper-right corner to close the note.

10. Open **OneNote 2013**. In the lower-left corner, click **Quick Notes.** On the right in the page navigation pane, select your note to open it.

You now know how to use **Send to OneNote**!

Chapter Summary

This chapter examined new features in OneNote 2013 using a hands-on approach. The improved searching capabilities were explored. You learned that searching is fast, almost instantaneous, and OneNote 2013 can search for just about any term you've captured.

New features supporting collaboration were explored, such as Sharing on SkyDrive, Get a Sharing Link (or Get a Link) and sharing notes during a meeting. You experienced how share permissions are granted to others using links.

OneNote 2013 has Mobile apps for all popular devices: Windows Phone, iOS devices, and Android phones. These can be downloaded from the app store for that device. If an app doesn't yet exist for your particular mobile device you can use an Internet browser to open your notes with the OneNote Web App!

On touch capable devices, OneNote 2013 has been enhanced so you can draw and edit with a finger or stylus. If you'd rather write than type, handwriting conversion in OneNote 2013 converts writing to text more accurately than previous versions.

You learned if you insert an Excel spreadsheet or a Visio object into OneNote 2013, you can edit those embedded files using the original application that created them (i.e., Excel or Visio). This assumes, of course, that you also have Excel or Visio installed on the device that is editing the object in OneNote 2013.

You discovered if you create a table in OneNote 2013, four new buttons appear on the Table Tools Layout contextual tab: Shading, Sort, and Convert to Excel Spreadsheet.

Finally, this chapter demonstrated how to use the new Send to OneNote utility. You experienced all three options: Screen Clipping, Send to OneNote, and New Quick Note. You learned these options allow you to send items to OneNote 2013 even when the application is not open.

Chapter 7:
New Features of
Outlook 2013

This chapter covers the following topics:

- ✓ Exchange ActiveSync Support
- ✓ Navigation Bar
- ✓ Peeks
- ✓ Social Network Connectors
- ✓ People Card
- ✓ Mail Enhancements
- ✓ Meeting Enhancements
- ✓ Weather Bar
- ✓ Improved Search

Outlook 2013 is included in all editions of Office 2013 except the traditional edition, Office Home and Student 2013. Outlook 2013 is one of the most powerful personal organizers on the market. Its features are no longer limited to working only with Microsoft Exchange servers. It is now possible to synchronize Contacts, Mail and Calendars with other popular email services, such as Hotmail. Social networking with Facebook and LinkedIn are also fully integrated into Outlook 2013.

This chapter will explain how Exchange ActiveSync can synchronize Outlook 2013 to other services. We will examine the new Navigation Bar and learn how Peeks provide convenient access to calendar and contact information. Social connectors to Facebook, LinkedIn, and Windows Live Messenger will be discussed. We will explore the new People Card, Mail Tips, and Inline Replies to email. We will see how to use Meeting Notes, Time Zones and Room Finder when setting up meetings. Last of all, this chapter will add the new Weather Bar to a calendar and explore the improved Search capabilities in Outlook 2013.

To master the new features presented in this chapter, you are encouraged to follow along with the hands-on demonstrations. You may use or create your own files; however, specific files are referenced in the instructions to help you master these features more quickly. Refer to Chapter One in this book for instructions on how to download the demonstration files.

Exchange ActiveSync Support

When connected to a Microsoft Exchange server, Outlook 2013 is a robust personal planner providing email, calendars, address books, and task lists to help you organize your life. Outlook 2013 can also connect to online email services using POP technology. Previous versions of Outlook could synchronize email with online services, but nothing else. Users of Hotmail, Gmail, and similar providers were often disappointed to discover their Calendars and Contacts could not be synchronized natively from within Outlook. A new feature of Outlook 2013 called Exchange ActiveSync has been designed to correct this shortfall.

Exchange ActiveSync makes it possible for Outlook 2013 to synchronize calendar appointments, contacts and email with many popular online services, such as Hotmail.com, Live.com and the new Outlook.com. Other services should be compatible in the future.

In this chapter, we will explore the new features of Outlook 2013 using fictitious email, contacts, people, and calendars that you won't want populating your personal or business email accounts. _Do not use your personal or business email account to perform the demonstrations in this book!_ Instead, this chapter will help you create a separate email account.

When you created your SkyDrive account in Chapter Two, a Hotmail account was simultaneously created for you. If you didn't create a SkyDrive account in Chapter Two, you will have the option to setup both accounts in this next demonstration.

Demonstration – Create a Hotmail.com Account

1. Go to **http://hotmail.com**

2. If you created a SkyDrive account in Chapter Two, use those same credentials to **login** to Hotmail, skip to step 4.

3. If you didn't create a SkyDrive account in Chapter Two, click **Sign up now** at the bottom of the screen. Complete the profile. When you finish, both a Hotmail and SkyDrive account will be setup for you.

4. You should now be in Hotmail[1].

[1]At the time this book was written, Hotmail was migrating to Outlook.com. If you were automatically redirected to Outlook.com, you can click the settings icon in the upper-right corner next to your login name to open a drop-down menu that will allow you to **Switch Back to Hotmail**. If you'd prefer to stay in Outlook.com, you can access Calendar, Contacts, Mail and SkyDrive by clicking the down arrow in the upper-left corner adjacent to the word **Outlook**.

5. **Create a calendar appointment:** In the menu at the top, hover over the word **Hotmail** to open a drop-down menu. In the drop-down menu, click **Calendar**.   This month's calendar will open. Choose a date about one week in the future and add the following appointment:
What*: Lunch with Boss*
Where: *My Favorite Restaurant*
Time: 12:00pm to 1:00pm.
Accept all other default settings. Click **Save**.

6. **Create a contact:** In the menu across the top, hover over the word **Hotmail** to open a drop-down menu. In the drop-down menu, click **Contacts**.   Click **+New** in the menu at the top. Enter the following:
First name*: Ray*
Last name: *Stone*
Company: Two Tire Tours
Email: *rstone@twotiretours.com*   Change the type to **Work**.
Work Phone: *(435) 123-4567*

Mobile Phone: *(435) 123-0098*
Home Address: *5431 Cliffside Ave., Moab, Utah 84532*
Work Address: *123 Rim Rock Blvd., Moab, Utah 84532*
Other (Title): *Sales/Tour Guide*
If necessary, use the vertical scroll on the right of your screen to reveal all the fields.   Click **Save**.

7. To **logout**, click your name in the upper-right corner then from the drop-down menu select **Sign out**.

What is Outlook.com?

July 31st, 2012 Microsoft introduced a preview of Outlook.com, an online service designed to eventually replace Windows Live Hotmail. Like SkyDrive and Hotmail, Outlook.com is free and has the following features:

- **Metro-style Interface** – navigation is easier with large fonts and graphical icons.

- **Integrated with Social Networks** – Outlook.com integrates with Facebook, Twitter, and LinkedIn so you can see profile pictures, messages, and status updates from contacts within Outlook 2013.

- **Fewer Ads** – like most free email services, Outlook.com is funded by ads, but the ads are pleasantly discrete. You only see the ad images if you hover over them.

- **Integrated with SkyDrive and Office Web Apps** – instead of sending photos and documents as enormous attachments, you can store the files onto your SkyDrive and email your viewers a link. In addition, Office Web Apps provides the tools necessary for your viewers to co-edit your documents, if you grant them permission.

- **Integrated with Skype** – Microsoft has announced they intend to integrate Outlook.com with Skype so you can communicate with your contacts in real-time using Instant Messaging, Voice and Video calls.

The following table compares Outlook.com to similar online services.

Table 5. Comparing Online Email Services

Security & Privacy	Outlook	Gmail	Hotmail
Keeps spam in your Inbox at less than 3%	•	•	•
SSL turned on by default	•	•	
View trusted senders in your Inbox	•	•	•
Doesn't serve targeted ads based on email contents	•		•
Modern Inbox			
Single attachment size per email	300 MB (SkyDrive)	25 MB	300 MB (SkyDrive)
Virtually unlimited storage (free)	•		•
Watch videos or slideshows from your Inbox	•	•	•
Share, view, and edit Microsoft Office docs using Office Web Apps	•		•
Send photo slide shows from your Inbox	•		•
Thread emails by conversation (optional)	•	•	•
Reading pane (optional)	•	*	•
Send mail from other email accounts	•	•	•
One click marks as read, delete, and filter from Inbox	•		•
Organizational Tools			
Create additional alias addresses to link to your Inbox	•		•
Organize Inbox by custom categories, folders, or both	•		•
Auto-categorize newsletters	•	*	•
Flag important messages to the top of your Inbox	•	•	•
Create time-based rules, such as "delete after 3 days"	•		•
Built-in search	•	•	•
Mobile Access			
Mobile access on major smartphones	•	•	•
Exchange ActiveSync (EAS)	•	•	•
POP aggregation	•	•	•
IMAP		•	
People			
Connect to Facebook, Twitter, and LinkedIn	•		
Chat with Facebook friends	•		•
Skype video call from your Inbox	**	***	

* Google Labs feature
** Coming soon
***Video chat using Google Chat

Source: http://windows.microsoft.com/en-US/windows/outlook-compare

Now that you've created an email account with a calendar appointment and a contact, you will connect Outlook 2013 and experience how Exchange ActiveSync smoothly synchronizes with online services.

Demonstration – Connecting Outlook 2013 to Hotmail

1. Launch **Outlook 2013**. If Outlook is not yet configured for an email account of any kind, skip the remainder of this step and go to step 2. Otherwise, select the **File** tab and click the **Account Settings** button. Select **Account Settings**. On the **E-mail** tab, click **New**…

2. When prompted to **Choose Service**, select **E-mail Account**.

3. In the **Auto Account Setup** window, select **Manual setup or additional server types**. Click **Next**.

4. In the Choose Service window, select **Outlook.com or Exchange ActiveSync compatible service.** Click **Next**.

5. In the **Server Settings** window, enter the following:
   Your Name: *The name you used for your new Hotmail account*
   E-mail Address: *Your-new-hotmail-username@hotmail.com*
   Mail Server: *m.hotmail.com*
   User Name: *Your-new-hotmail-username*
   Password: *Your-new-hotmail-password*
   Enable the checkbox **Remember password**. Click **Next**.

6. After Outlook completes testing your account settings, click **Close**. Click **Finish**. If you are returned to **Account Settings**, click **Close**.

7. Your Hotmail email address should appear in the Outlook 2013 folder pane. Click the expansion arrow to see your email folders.

8. In the lower left of the Outlook 2013 window, click **Calendar**. Verify your Hotmail calendar synchronized by viewing *Lunch Appointment with Boss* created in the **Demonstration – Create a Hotmail.com Account**.

9. In the lower left of the Outlook 2013 window, click **People**. Verify your Hotmail contacts synchronized by viewing the card you created for *Ray Stone* in the **Demonstration – Create a Hotmail.com Account**.

Navigation Bar

The Navigation Pane which resided on the left side of Outlook 2007 and Outlook 2010 has been simplified in Outlook 2013. It is now simply a Folder Pane supporting just email. Replacing the old Navigation Pane is a Navigation Bar that has the words **Mail**, **Calendar**, **People**, and **Tasks** displayed across the bottom of the Outlook 2013 window. If you prefer icons instead of words, you can customize the Navigation Bar.

Demonstration – Customizing the Navigation Bar

1. Outlook 2013 should be open from the previous demonstration. If not, open it.

2. Select the **File** tab, click **Options**. Select **Advanced**.

3. Under the **Outlook Panes** section, click the **Navigation** button.

4. Explore the options. You can configure how many items appear in the Navigation bar. If you select Compact Navigation, icons will be displayed instead of words. You can also control their order.

5. When you've finished exploring the **Navigation Options**, click **OK**.

Peeks

Another new feature of Outlook 2013 is something Microsoft is calling "Peeks". Simply hover over **Calendar**, **People**, or **Tasks** on the Navigation Bar and a window will pop-up that allows you to conveniently view your monthly calendar, search contacts, or see a list of active tasks. You no longer need to leave what you're doing in Outlook 2013 to access this information; instead you can conveniently peek at it!

Demonstration – Using Peeks

1. Outlook 2013 should be open from the previous demonstration. If not, open it.

2. On the **Navigation** Bar located at the bottom of the window, hover over **Calendar**, **People** and **Tasks** to see each Peek window.

3. In the **People** Peek, you can search. Type, *Ray Stone*. You should see the contact you created in this chapter's first demonstration.

Social Network Connectors

Outlook 2013 has built-in integration for Facebook, LinkedIn, SharePoint and Windows Live Messenger. Microsoft claims they will add support for other providers as they become available[1]. If you participate in one or more of these social networks, adding them to Outlook 2013 allows you to view profile pictures, messages, and status updates from your contacts without leaving Outlook.

Adding a Social Network is easy. If you change your mind later, it is just as easy to delete a Social Network Account.

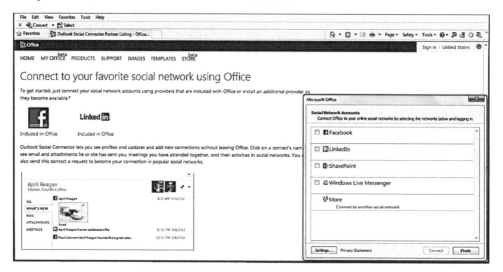

[1] Source: http://office.microsoft.com/en-us/outlook/outlook-social-connector-partner-listing-FX102921430.aspx

Demonstration – Adding Social Networks Accounts

1. Outlook 2013 should already be open. If not, open it.

2. To add Social Networking Accounts, select the **File** tab and click on **Account Settings**.   Click **Social Networking Accounts**.

3. Check the box of the Social Network to add (i.e., Facebook). This will expand the item so you can add your login information. You may also check the box to show photos. When finished, click **Connect**.

4. To change the settings or remove a Social Network, click either the **Edit** or **Delete** icon in the upper-right next to the connection name.

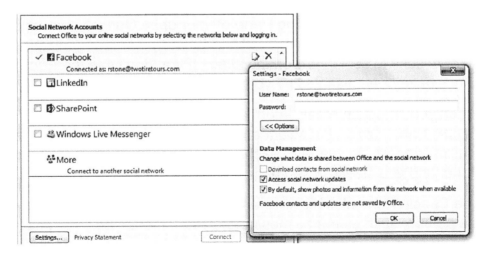

5. When you are done adding Social Connections, click **Finished**.

An alternate way to access Social Network Accounts is from the **People Pane** button on the **View** tab.

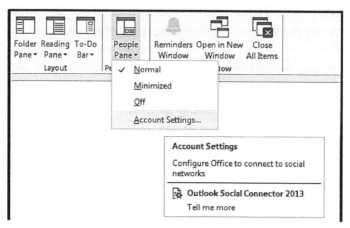

How Social Connections Display Information

The Outlook Social Connector lets you work in Outlook 2013 while staying up to date on the status and activities of your friends and colleagues, whether they're within your organization or from Facebook or LinkedIn. Information is updated in your Outlook People contacts whenever a friend or colleague changes their profile on their social network. For example, if one of your friends or colleagues changes a photo on their profile, the photo will likewise be changed in your Outlook People contacts.

The Outlook Social Connector sends information to the People Pane, which sits below the Reading Pane of your open Outlook item, such as an e-mail, appointment, or contact. Unfortunately, some organizations don't allow access to social networking sites. If you don't see the People pane, it may have been disabled by your IT Department.

When you select an email, information about the sender appears in the People Pane. When you select an Outlook 2013 item that includes multiple people, an image of each person appears at the top of the People Pane, and you can click an image to display detailed information for each.

The People Pane also displays a list of all Outlook activity you've had with the person, such as e-mail messages, attachments, and meetings.

How the Outlook Social Connector works

The following is an excerpt from the Microsoft legal statement about how the Outlook Social Connector functions:

> ### Details on how the Outlook Social Connector works
>
> *When viewing an e-mail message in Outlook, the Outlook Social Connector displays information such as past messages and attachments from the people in that Conversation. If a connection to a social network exists and you are logged into that social network, the Outlook Social Connector may ask the social network for information about those people. Information can include photos, status updates, activity feeds, and profile information (name, title, e-mail address, etc.).*
>
> *Depending on the choices made by the creators of the social network add-in, when viewing a message, the Outlook Social Connector may ask the social network for information about everyone on the To and Cc lines of the message. The e-mail addresses for those people are hashed before they are sent to the social network to prevent disclosure of email addresses. Social networks can only match an e-mail address of a person who is already known on the social network. They may also decide to save the information in Outlook for your offline use. For more information about third-party privacy practices, contact the third-party add-in provider or read their privacy statement.*

Source: http://office.microsoft.com/en-us/outlook/learn-more-about-outlook-social-connector-and-privacy-HA101880243.aspx

People Card

Adding multiple email accounts and social networking accounts to Outlook 2013 can create duplicate contact cards. Outlook 2013 automatically merges contact cards for the same person into a single Peeks view called a "People Card". The People Card collects all the key details about a contact in one place: phone, email, address, company info, even social media updates when available.

All of the person's contact information is under the tab **Contacts**, which is displayed by default. From the **Contacts** tab, you can schedule a meeting, send an instant message, email, or call the person on the phone.

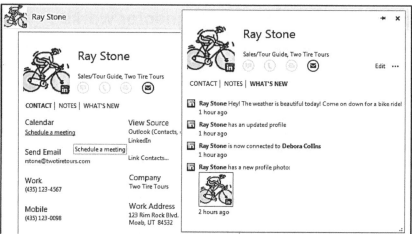

Social Network updates from this person can be viewed by clicking on the **What's New** tab. The People Card conveniently brings all available information about a person into a single view!

Mail Enhancements

Two very useful features have been added to email. Both will save you time. One can even save you from an occasional embarrassment.

In-line Replies

Office 2013 allows you to reply to an email without opening it! You can now **Reply**, **Reply All** or **Forward** from within the **Reading Pane**. Of course, you can still open each email and respond the traditional way, but this feature provides a method for quicker handling of large volumes of mail from within the **Reading Pane**.

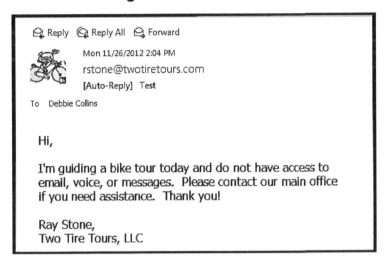

Mail Tips

Mail Tips were introduced with Outlook 2010, but they've been enhanced in Outlook 2013. Have you ever composed an email with instructions about an attachment and then forget to send the attachment? Or replied to a group, and then discovered the group contained hundreds of recipients! We've all been embarrassed by at least one of these mistakes. Outlook 2013 helps prevent email errors from happening. Mail Tips is a dialog box that warns you about common mistakes, such as forgetting to attach a document, or forgetting that your email recipient is on vacation, or that the recipient is a large group, and other useful warnings.

Mail Tips require that you be attached to an Exchange Server. Network administrators in companies that use Exchange Server can configure Mail

Tips to help enforce policies. Policy tips can notify employees if their email messages contain sensitive information governed by company security or data-handling policies. For example, warnings can pop up if the email contains a credit card number or if an employee attempts to send sensitive information to someone outside the organization. Mail Tips can help raise employee awareness regarding email content.

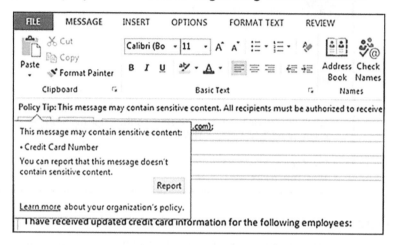

The Hotmail account you created for use with this book does not support Mail Tips. To verify if one of your personal or business accounts supports Mail Tips, launch Outlook 2010 or 2013 for that account and go to Options under the **File** tab, select **Mail** and scroll down the list. **Mail Tips** should appear between the **Send Messages** and **Tracking** sections.

Meeting Enhancements

A few new features have been added to the business editions and the Office Professional Plus 2013 edition of Outlook.

- **Lync Meeting** – sets up a Lync Meeting as easily as scheduling a regular meeting. The meeting link and call-in phone numbers are automatically added to the meeting request.

- **Meeting Notes** – allows you to add notes to the meeting using OneNote or open notes already associated with the meeting.

- **Time Zones** – adds a time zone field to the meeting Start/End time.

- **Room Finder**[1] – opens a list of available rooms (configured on the Exchange Server), a monthly calendar and list of suggested times.

[1] If you're not connected to an Exchange Server, this button will not be visible.

Demonstration – Adding Time Zones and Meeting Notes

1. Outlook 2013 should be open from a previous demonstration. If not, open it.

2. On the **Navigation Bar**, click **Calendar**. On the **Home** tab, click **New Meeting**.

3. In the **Options** group, click the **Time Zones** button. This will add time zones to the right of the **Start Time:** and **End Time:** fields.

4. Create a meeting invitation with the following:

   To: *rstone@twotiretours.com*
   Subject: *Spring Bike Tour*
   Location: *Conference Call*
   Start Time: *Choose tomorrow's date, 9:00am, Mountain Time*
   End Time: *Choose tomorrow's date, 9:30am, Mountain Time*
   Message: *Hi, Ray! Let's discuss details of our bike ride!*

5. Click the **Meeting Notes** button, then **Share notes with the meeting**. If the notebook window is empty, complete **Chapter 6 Demonstration – Sharing a Notebook on SkyDrive**, steps 1 – 5.

6. Next to the **TwoTireTours** notebook, click the **+** symbol to expand it.

7. Select the **Miscellaneous** section (select the section, not the page).

8. Outlook 2013 will embed a link in your meeting invitation. Click the link to see the page. Notice that Outlook 2013 automatically creates a page in your online notebook with the meeting details (i.e., subject, date, time, location and a list of participants).

9. Return to Outlook 2013 and send your meeting request! If you receive a notice from Hotmail, ignore it. You're done!

Weather Bar

A new feature to Calendars in Outlook 2013 is the Weather Bar. This feature provides a simple three-day forecast for any location you configure. The temperature can be displayed in either Fahrenheit or Celsius. Why would you need a Weather Bar? Well, it can be very useful when planning special appointments, such as meetings on the golf course!

Demonstration – Adding a Weather Bar to Calendars

1. Outlook 2013 should be open from a previous demonstration. If not, open it.

2. Under the **File** tab, click **Options**, and select **Calendar**.

3. Scroll to the bottom of the list of Calendar options.

4. Enable the checkbox, **Show weather on the calendar**. Select if you'd like the temperature displayed in **Celsius** or **Fahrenheit**.

5. Click **OK**.

6. On the **Navigation Bar**, click **Calendar**.

7. The Weather Bar should display a city and a 3-day forecast across the top of your calendar. To change the city, click the down-arrow and select **Add Location**.

8. Enter either a city name or zip code (best). Click the Search magnifying glass, and then select the city name that best matches.

Improved Search

In Outlook 2013, you can locate information in email, attachments, calendar appointments, and contacts through an improved search engine.

In this final demonstration, we will explore searching a calendar, and then we will see how to search through all Outlook items simultaneously.

Demonstration – Searching Outlook Items

1. Before completing this demonstration, you must first complete the **Demonstration – Adding Time Zones and Meeting Notes.**

2. On the **Navigation Bar**, click **Calendar**.

3. In the **Search** field located in the upper-right corner type, *Bike*. A search result should display for the meeting you created in the previous demonstration.

4. On the **Navigation Bar**, click **Mail**.

5. In the **Search** field type, *Bike*. In the adjacent field to the right, click **Current Mailbox** and change the search criteria to **All Outlook Items**.

6. Results should display in the sections **Calendar** and **Sent Items.**

7. When you have finished exploring Search, close Outlook 2013 by clicking the **File** tab and clicking **Exit**.

Chapter Summary

This chapter explored the new features of Outlook 2013 using a hands-on approach. It explained how Exchange ActiveSync makes it possible for Outlook 2013 to synchronize calendar appointments, contacts and email with many popular online services, such as Hotmail. Outlook.com was introduced as the new Microsoft email service designed to replace Hotmail. Its planned features were compared to Gmail and Hotmail.

A new Navigation Bar was examined and a new feature called Peeks. You learned that when you hover over Calendar, People, or Tasks on the Navigation Bar a pop-up window appears that allows you to conveniently peek at your calendar, search contacts, or see a list of active tasks.

Outlook 2013 has built-in integration for Facebook, LinkedIn, SharePoint and Windows Live Messenger. You learned how the Outlook Social Connector enables you to connect to these social networks to view profile pictures, messages, and status updates from your contacts without leaving Outlook 2013.

When contact information is obtained from multiple sources, multiple contact cards are produced. Outlook 2013 overcomes this issue by automatically merging information onto a single People Card. This card collects all the key details about a contact in one place: phone, email, address, company info, even social media updates when available. The People Card is a Peek viewed by hovering over People on the Navigation Bar.

Two enhancements to email were explored. The first was In-line Replies which allows you to reply to an email from within the Reading Pane. The second was Mail Tips which is a dialog box that warns you about common email mistakes, such as forgetting to attach a document.

Four new buttons on the Meetings tab were examined: Lync Meeting, Meeting Notes, Time Zones, and Room Finder.

Last of all, this chapter demonstrated the new Weather Bar for Calendars, and the improved Search capabilities of Outlook 2013.

Chapter 8:
New Features of
Access 2013

This chapter covers the following topics:

- ✓ App Templates
- ✓ Table Templates
- ✓ Drill and Peek
- ✓ Autocomplete
- ✓ Data Storage and Control

Access is an application used to build databases. It is included in all editions of Office 2013 except the traditional editions of Office Home and Student, and Office Home and Business. Access installs on a PC only, not a Mac or tablet device.

If you're an Access lover, you may be disappointed to learn it received very few enhancements in this new version of Office. On the other hand, you may be excited to discover that the new features it did receive make it very easy to build web-based databases, even if you have no knowledge of programming!

Since there are very few enhancements to Access 2013, this chapter is short. It begins by introducing new templates to support web-app development. Drill and Peek, and Autocomplete will be explained as new features for searching online Access databases. Finally, this chapter concludes with an examination of Data Storage and Control for web-based Access 2013 databases.

To create a web-app in Access, you need two components: Access 2013 and rights to a SharePoint Server 2013. Since most readers of this book won't have an edition of Office that includes SharePoint 2013, there are no demonstrations in this chapter. However, this chapter does explain how easy it is to create web-apps using Access 2013. If you have SharePoint 2013, feel free to follow along with the general steps provided in this chapter and you can still obtain a hands-on experience.

App Templates

Access has been used for many years to create desktop databases, but "desktop" databases are not the focus of the enhancements made to Access 2013. Remember our discussion in Chapter Two about Microsoft encouraging users of Office 2013 to transition to cloud-based computing? The new Access conforms to this philosophy. The improvements in Access 2013 support developing apps that run within a web browser, not the desktop. Both the app and the database reside on a SharePoint Server 2013 connected to the Internet.

Access 2013 contains App Templates for the most common databases needed by people, such as Asset Tracking, Contacts, Issue Tracking, Project Management, and Task Management. If none of these templates fit your need, there is also a Custom Web App Template.

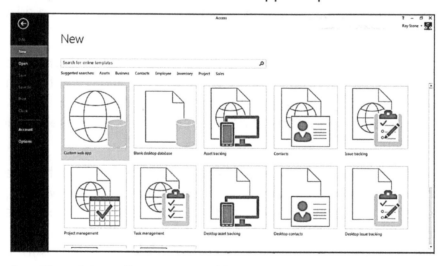

These App Templates allow a user with no knowledge of programming to build databases on a SharePoint server that can be accessed with a web browser. The Access 2013 web app creates the entire database structure, complete with views (previously called, "forms" in desktop databases) that allow users to add and edit data. Navigation and basic commands are built-in, so the web app can be shared and used right away. This simplicity of creating online databases allows businesses to focus on building and sharing data without worry about programming logistics.

Let's explore how easy this is by walking through the steps of creating a basic web-app database using the built-in App Templates. Follow along if you have rights to a SharePoint 2013 server.

General Steps to Create a Web-App Database

1. Launch Access 2013.

2. On the Access startup screen, scroll to see the featured web-app templates: **Custom Web App**, **Asset Tracking**, **Contacts**, **Issue Tracking**, **Project Management**, and **Task Management**.

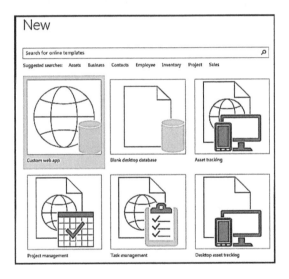

3. Click **Custom Web App**. Enter the following:
App Name: *My New App*
Web Location: http://*YourSharePointAddress.com*
Click the **Create** button.

4. Access will take a few moments to create the database structure.

Table Templates

Access 2013 also has new Table Templates to support the web-apps. Once you've created a web-app database, the next step is to add tables. The Table Templates create the fields and views (formerly called "forms) that organize your data and make it accessible. You can add pre-defined tables using these templates, or you can build from blank tables.

General Steps to Add Tables to a Web-App Database

1. Once the App Template builds the database, you'll be prompted to add Tables. Tables are used to track data - Orders, Customers, Products, Suppliers - anything you want. Access 2013 has many pre-defined tables that are commonly needed.

2. If you want to track Orders, type *Orders* into the search field. A list of related templates will be displayed. Click the **Orders** template.

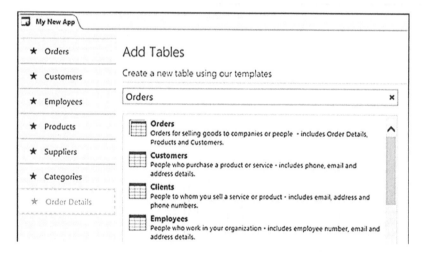

3. Once you've selected a template, Access 2013 will automatically create the tables, fields and views (formerly called, "forms").

4. When you are finished designing your tables, you don't need to Save or Publish your web-app because it is already live! Simply go to the **Home** tab and click the **Launch App** button.

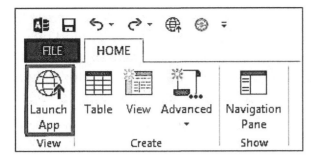

5. The Launch App button opens your browser so you can begin entering data!

Drill and Peek

If a record in a web-app has a Lookup field, the data it references can be displayed as a hyperlink to another table. Clicking the hyperlink allows you to "Drill" down and pop open a form displaying the detailed data. This pop-up form provides a "Peek" at the relevant information in the database without requiring the user to change views away from the parent view.

Autocomplete

By default, all List Views created in an Access 2013 web-app include a Search Box. When you begin typing data in the Search box, drop-down menus containing recommendations appear to help you make accurate entries. There is no code needed to create this Search Box. It's built automatically and included in the view (i.e., form) by default!

Data Storage and Control

When you created a web application in Access 2010, the tables were stored as SharePoint lists on the SharePoint 2010 server. This is not the case with Access 2013.

In Access 2013, when you create a web-app on a SharePoint server, Access Services creates a SQL Server or SQL Azure database that houses all of the objects and data that your app requires. The tables, queries, macros, and forms are all stored in this database.

If you create the app on a SharePoint server that your company hosts, Access creates the database on the SQL Server designated by your SharePoint server. If you create your app in Office 365, the database is created in SQL Azure. In either case, the database created is specific to your app and is not shared with other apps on the storage server.

The role of the SQL Server or SQL Azure server is to ensure data integrity, and provide disaster recovery and back-up/restore services for your data. Either of these servers increases performance and scalability of your database when compared to traditional desktop storage. It also allows you the opportunity to have SQL developers work with your data.

The role of the SharePoint 2013 server is to provide user access control and management for your Access 2013 web-app. Permissions granted to other users to view data; or add, modify, or remove data; is controlled by the SharePoint 2013 server. When you create a web app in Access 2013, you must designate a SharePoint site where you want it to live. The app can be accessed, managed, or uninstalled from this site just like any other SharePoint app.

Chapter Summary

This chapter examined the new features of Access 2013. The features focus very little on the database aspects of Access and almost entirely on its capabilities as a development tool for web-based database apps.

App Templates are new to Access 2013. Templates exist to create the most common databases: Asset Tracking, Contacts, Issue Tracking, Project Management, and Task Management. There is also a Custom Web App Template.

Once the web-app database is created, you can add Table Templates, which automatically create the tables, fields and views.

There is no need to publish an Access 2013 web-app; it is live as soon as it is created.

New features for working with data are Drill and Peak, and Autocomplete. Drill and Peek allow a user to see relevant information in the database without changing views away from the parent view. Autocomplete aids you when typing.

Finally, this chapter explained that SQL Server or SQL Azure Server ensures data integrity, disaster recovery, back-up and restore for your Access 2013 web-app database. If you create the app on a SharePoint server that your company hosts, Access creates the database on the SQL Server designated by your SharePoint server. If you create your app in Office 365, the database is created in SQL Azure. In either case, each database created is specific to the app and not shared with other apps on the server.

A SharePoint 2013 server is required to provide user control and management for the web-app.

Chapter 9:
New Features of
Publisher 2013

This chapter covers the following topics:

- ✓ Templates
- ✓ WordArt
- ✓ Scratch Area
- ✓ Live Picture Swap
- ✓ Picture Backgrounds
- ✓ Save for Photo Printing

Publisher is included in all editions of Office 2013 except the traditional editions of Office Home and Student, and Office Home and Business 2013. Several enhancements have been added to Publisher 2013 including more templates, improved styles and text effects, a general scratch area for importing multiple pictures, several tools for editing images, and better support for exporting projects for commercial printing.

This chapter introduces the new template pane in Publisher 2013. The addition of WordArt Styles is explored. New features supporting images are examined: Scratch Area, Live Picture Swap, and saving pictures as background images. Last of all, this chapter explores a new feature for saving publications in formats ready for printing at a photo center.

To master the new features presented in this chapter, you are encouraged to follow along with the hands-on demonstrations. You may use or create your own files; however, specific files are referenced in the instructions to help you master these features more quickly. Refer to Chapter One in this book for instructions on how to download the demonstration files.

Templates

Microsoft has expanded the number of templates available in Publisher 2013. You'll now find a greater variety of templates to help you create labels, flyers, invitations, calendars, business cards, certificates, signs, brochures, newsletters, and other common documents.

Demonstration – Using Templates in Publisher 2013

1. Launch Publisher 2013. The redesigned template pane will open. Several **FEATURED** templates are displayed in this pane. Click the word **BUILT-IN** located directly above the templates. These are all of the templates available to you while offline. Among the built-in templates that are displayed, click **Brochures**.

2. Choose one of the brochures on the first row. The pane on the far right allows you to customize the template by changing the **Color Scheme**, **Font Scheme** and **Business Information**. You can also change the layout from **3-panel** to **4-panel**, enable a checkbox to **Include customer address**, and add one of three forms to one of the panels (i.e., **Order form**, **Response form**, **Sign-up form**).

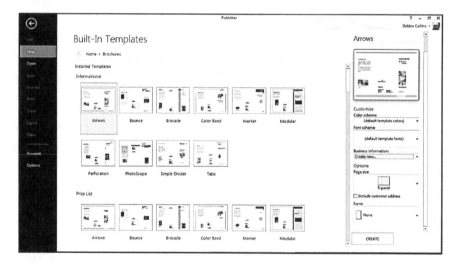

3. When you have finished exploring, click the word **Home** located at the top of the screen below the title **Built-In Templates**.

4. Across the top of the template pane is a **Search** field that allows you to search Office.com for online templates. Type, *Brochure* and press **Enter** or click the **Search** icon (magnifying glass). A large number of brochure templates will be displayed.

5. You can scroll through the results in the main template pane or view the results organized by **Category** using the pane on the far right.

6. Select one of the templates. It will be displayed in the center of your screen. **Left and right arrows**, at the bottom of the displayed template, allow you to navigate through the template page layouts.

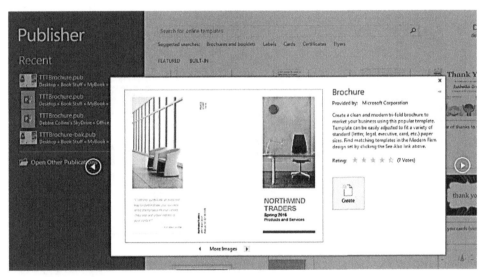

7. When you have finished exploring templates, click the word **Home** located at the top of the screen to the left of the **Search** field.

WordArt

The new version of "WordArt", which was also added to Word 2013, is now available in Publisher 2013. The **WordArt Styles** in Publisher 2013 allow you to manipulate three features: **Text Fills**, **Text Outlines**, and **Text Effects**. You can combine these three features manually, or choose from fifteen (15) pre-defined combinations called **WordArt Styles**.

Demonstration – Adding WordArt

1. In Publisher 2013, select **File>Open**. Select the location where you unzipped the demonstration files you downloaded in Chapter One (i.e., SkyDrive or Computer). **Browse** *toTTTBrochure.pub*. Select it and click the **Open** button.

2. In the **Pages** pane on the left, select page **1** of the brochure.

3. Select the text in the right panel of the brochure, **Two Tire Tours**. The contextual tabs, **Drawing Tools** and **Text Box Tools** will appear.

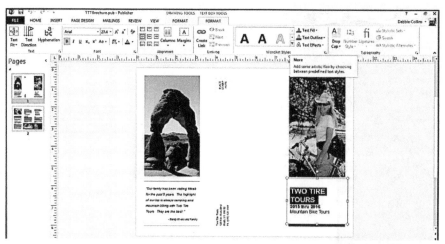

4. Select the **Text Box Tools Format** contextual tab. Everything in the **WordArt Styles** group is new to Publish 2013. Open the pre-defined text styles gallery by clicking the drop-down menu. Hover over each of the 15 pre-defined styles to see how they affect your selected text.

5. To the right of the gallery are three drop-down menus for **Text Fill**, **Outline Fill** and **Text Effects**. Spend a few minutes exploring each.

6. In the bottom right corner of the **WordArt Styles** group, click the dialog box launcher (i.e., the little arrow labeled **"Text Fill Effects"**). Take a few minutes to explore the options available in this dialog box.

7. When finished, click outside the publication to deselect the text.

Scratch Area

Replacing and switching images is easier in Publisher 2013 than in previous versions. Previous versions required images to be inserted one at a time. In Publisher 2013, you can import multiple images simultaneously. Two buttons are available for importing images; both are located under the **Insert** tab in the **Illustrations** group. The first button is the **Pictures** button, which allows you to insert images stored on your local device or a local network. The second button, which was called "ClipArt" in previous versions of Publisher, has been renamed **Online Pictures** in Publisher 2013. The **Online Pictures** button allows you to obtain images from the Internet or your SkyDrive.

Rather than stacking all imported images onto the center of your page, like in previous versions of Publisher, the images are now placed in a workspace located to the right of your project called a "Scratch Area". The **Scratch Area** displays thumbnails of your images until you either use them or delete them.

Demonstration – Importing Images onto the Scratch Area

1. If you just completed the previous demonstration in this chapter, skip this step. Otherwise, in Publisher 2013 select **File>Open**. Select the location where you unzipped the demonstration files you downloaded in Chapter One (i.e., SkyDrive or Computer). **Browse** to *TTTBrochure.pub*. Select it and click the **Open** button.

2. On the **Insert** tab, click the appropriate button to access the area where you unzipped the demonstration files: the **Pictures** button will allow you to browse your Computer; the **Online Pictures** button will allow you to browse your SkyDrive.

3. Select the following images simultaneously: **Barrier Canyon.JPG**, **Cactus Flower.JPG**, and **Newspaper Rock.JPG**. Click **Insert**.

4. The thumbnails of three images should simultaneously appear in a workspace to the right of the document - this is the **Scratch Area**.

Live Picture Swap

There are a couple of ways you can change pictures in a publication. Live Picture Swap provides the quickest way. Simply drag an image from the scratch area until it's over an existing image and a pink highlight appears over the existing image. The two images will instantly switch places.

A second method is to select both the image you want to replace and the replacement image. A **Picture Swap** icon will appear in the center of the selected image. Clicking this icon swaps the two images.

A third option is to select both the image you want to replace and the replacement image, then click the **Swap** button on the **Picture Tools Format** tab.

When Live Picture Swap is used to exchange images, the formatting of the image on the document is unaltered, such as size, borders or effects. The replacement image will automatically inherit these properties.

Demonstration – Using Live Picture Swap

1. This demonstration requires that you complete the previous **Demonstration – Importing Images onto the Scratch Area.** On the first page of the brochure, select the image **Delicate Arch**.

2. In the **Pages** pane on the left, select the page **1** of the brochure.

3. Select the **Cactus Flower** thumbnail as the replacement image.

   Note: If you are using a PC, hold down the **CTRL** key to select multiple images. If you are using a Mac, hold down **COMMAND (Apple)** key. Selecting multiple images on a tablet device varies on devices. On the Microsoft Surface, swipe up and a checkmark will appear on each image to indicate they are selected.

4. Hover over one of the two selected images to reveal the **Swap** icon. Click the **Swap** icon. An alternate option is to click the **Swap** button on the **Picture Tools Format** tab. The images should trade places.

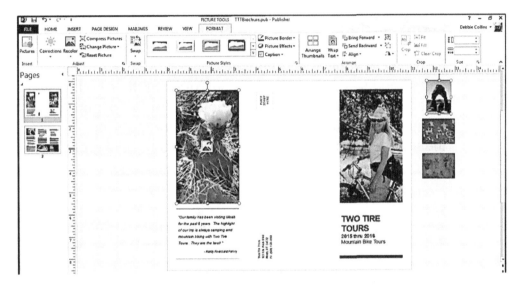

5. When finished exploring Live Picture Swap. Use the **Undo** button in the **Quick Access Toolbar** above the Ribbon to restore the document to its original state.

Picture Backgrounds

Publisher 2013 provides more options than Publisher 2010, for saving a picture as a background. When using the **Apply Image** button on the **Page Design** tab, you can now choose to use the image as a fill and set its transparency; or tile the image and control aspects of the tiling. These new features can also be accessed by right-clicking an image and selecting **Apply to Background**.

Demonstration – Setting an Image as Background

1. This demonstration requires that you complete the previous **Demonstration – Importing Images onto the Scratch Area.** On the first page of the brochure, select the image **Delicate Arch**.

2. In the **Pages** pane on the left, select the page **1** of the brochure.

3. In the **Scratch Area**, select the thumbnail of the **Barrier Canyon** photo (light brown with reddish images). Right-click and select **Format Picture**. Set the **Transparency** to **30%**. Click **OK**.

4. One way to apply the image as a background is to right-click the image and select **Apply to Background>Fill**. Another way is to select the image and from the **Picture Tools Format** tab, in the **Page Background** group, click **Apply Image>Fill**. Choose one of these methods and apply the image as a fill background.

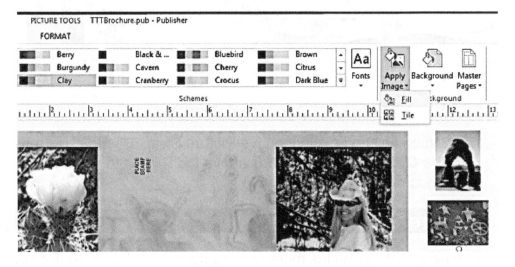

5. The image should now appear as a faded background on page 1.

6. In the **Pages** pane on the left, select the page **2** of the brochure.

7. In the **Scratch Area**, select the thumbnail of the **Newspaper Rock** photo (light black background with brown images). On the **Page**

Design tab, in the **Page Background** group, click **Background,** and then click **More Backgrounds…**

8. All options can be set from this single **Format Background** box. Click **Picture or Texture Fill**. Notice the buttons allow you to import images from **File…, Clipboard…** or **Online…** directly from this dialog box. Click **File**. Browse to select **Newspaper Rock.JPG**. You can also configure the Transparency level and Tiling. For this demonstration, set the **Transparency** to **70%**, accept all other settings, and click **OK**.

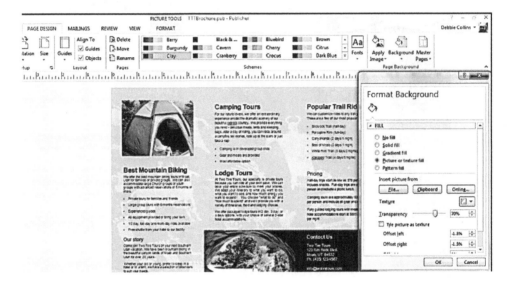

9. The image should now appear as a faded background on page 2.

Save for Photo Printing

A new feature called **Save for Photo Printing** can be found under the File tab, in **Export**, within the **Pack and Go** section. This feature saves each page of your document as either a JPEG or TIFF image, which is ideal if you want to package your publication to print at a photo center.

Demonstration – Package Publication for Photo Printing

1. If you just completed the previous demonstrations in this chapter, skip this step. Otherwise, in Publisher 2013 select **File>Open**.

Select the location where you unzipped the demonstration files you downloaded in Chapter One (i.e., SkyDrive or Computer). **Browse** to*TTTBrochure.pub*. Select it and click the **Open** button.

2. Select the **File** tab and click **Export**. Under **Pack and Go**, click the new feature called, **Save for Photo Printing**.

3. Files printed at a photo center typically must be in a JPEG or TIFF format. This feature saves each page of your publication as a separate image file and packages them into a folder. For this demonstration, select **JPEG Images for Photo Printing**. Click **Save Image Set**.

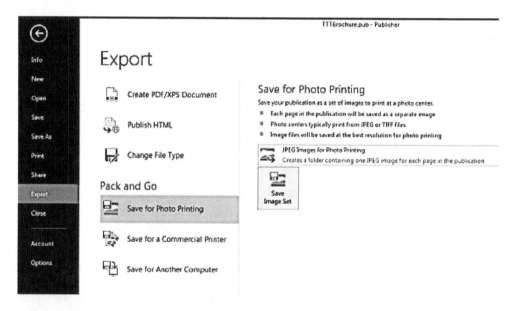

4. Browse up a level and save the file in the **Office 2013 DemoFiles** folder. Click **Select Folder**. Wait a few moments while Publisher 2013 generates the files. A new folder will be created using the same name as the .pub file, **TTTBrochure**.

5. Browse to locate the new **TTTBrochure** folder. Open it to verify the publication has been saved as two JPG files.

6. This folder is now ready to be printed at a Photo Center.

Chapter Summary

This chapter examined new features of Publisher 2013 using a hands-on approach. New online templates were introduced to enhance the selection of built-in templates that existed in previous versions. These templates can be used to create labels, flyers, invitations, calendars, business cards, certificates, signs, brochures, newsletters, and other common documents.

The same WordArt that was added to Word 2013 is now available in Publisher 2013. WordArt allows you to apply Text Fills, Text Outlines, and Text Effects. These WordArt features can be applied separately, or from a gallery of fifteen (15) pre-defined combinations called WordArt Styles.

Multiple images can now be imported simultaneously into Publisher 2013, and are automatically placed into a Scratch Area. The new Scratch Area is a workspace that holds imported images until they are either deleted or placed onto the publication.

Live Picture Swap is used to exchange an image in a document with a replacement image in the Scratch Area. All formatting properties of the original image (i.e., size, borders, and effects) are automatically inherited by the replacement image.

Publisher 2013 has an Apply Image button on the Page Design tab, in the Page Background group, that allows you to use an image as a background fill and set its transparency; or tile the image in the background and control aspects of the tiling.

Finally, this chapter examined Save for Photo Printing, which is a new feature that saves each page of the publication as either a JPEG or TIFF image so it can be printed at a photo center.

Appendix 1: Technical Information for IT Professionals

This Appendix covers the following topics:

- ✓ 32-bit vs. 64-bit version of Office
- ✓ Active Directory-Based Activation
- ✓ Apps for Office
- ✓ Click-to-Run Customization
- ✓ Managing Office 2013 with Group Policy
- ✓ Office Telemetry Dashboard and Log
- ✓ Office Web Apps
- ✓ Office Web Apps Server
- ✓ Security Changes
- ✓ Sign-in IDs

This Appendix contains articles and excerpts collected from Microsoft websites for your convenience. The information is subject to change. Please check the source hyperlinks to verify if updates have been made.

32-bit vs. 64-bit version of Office

In most cases, install the 32-bit version of Microsoft Office. We recommend the 32-bit version of Office because it helps prevent compatibility issues with other applications, especially third-party add-ins. We also recommend that you install Silverlight together with Office 2013 to improve the online experience.

Office installs the 32-bit version automatically even if your computer is running 64-bit editions of Windows. You might want to install the 64-bit version of Office if you usually work with extra-large databases or worksheets or develop for the 64-bit platform.

If you already have a 64-bit version of Office installed on your computer running a 64-bit operating system, 64-bit version is automatically installed.

What's included in the 64-bit version of Office?

Most things in the 32-bit version are in the 64-bit version of Office.

The following are some things not in the 64-bit version of Office.

- **ActiveX controls library, ComCtl**   This library contains ActiveX controls used to build solutions. It is most commonly used in Microsoft Access, Microsoft Excel, and Microsoft Word.

- **SharePoint List control**   The list view in SharePoint Technology isn't available in 64-bit version of Office.

Compatibility with existing Office files and solutions

The 64-bit version of Microsoft Office isn't compatible with any other 32-bit version of Office programs. So you must first uninstall all 32-bit versions of Office programs before you install the 64-bit version of Office. The Office disc includes both 32- and 64-bit versions. To install 64-bit Office, you must run Setup.exe from the x64 folder. For more information, see the **Install the 64-bit version of Office** section below.

- **ActiveX controls library, ComCtl** - Any solutions using these controls doesn't work. No good alternatives are available for some of these controls.

- **Third-party ActiveX controls and add-ins** - None of these work with the 64-bit version of Office.

    Note: There is no 64-bit version of Visual Basic 6, so many of these objects need to be ported and rewritten.

- **Microsoft Visual Basic for Applications (VBA)** - VBA only contains the Declare statement work in the 64-bit version of Office if you update the code manually.

- **Compiled Access databases** - The .MDE and .ACCDE files, a common way for Access application developers to distribute solutions and protect their intellectually property, don't work in the 64-bit version of Office. You must contact the application developer to recompile, retest, and redistribute the solution in the 64-bit version.

Operating systems required to run 64-bit version of Office

Your computer must be running at least 64-bit edition Windows 7, Windows Server 7, or Windows 8.

Install the 64-bit version of Office

Important: If you already have a 64-bit version of Office installed on your computer running a 64-bit operating system, running Setup from the root folder installs the 64-bit version of Office.

Any add-ins you want to run for Office must also be 64-bit editions.

During Setup

1. If you ran Office Setup from the root folder and you clicked **Customize**, click **Close** to exit Setup.

2. Click **Yes** to cancel Setup, and then click **Close**.

3. Go to the x64 folder on the Office disc, and double-click **Setup.exe** to run the 64-bit version of Setup.

From My Account

1. Go to http://office.microsoft.com/en-us/signin.aspx

2. Click **Language** and **Install Options > Additional Install Options > Office 64-bit > Install**.

Source: http://officepreview.microsoft.com/en-us/support/choose-the-32-bit-or-64-bit-version-of-office-HA102840825.aspx

Active Directory-Based Activation

Volume activation establishes a relationship between the Volume License (VL) product key and a particular installation of the VL software on a device. Microsoft policy requires you to activate VL editions of Office 2010 and Office 2013 that run on both physical computers and virtual machines.

When Office 2013 runs on Windows 8 or Windows Server 2012, a new volume activation method is available: Active Directory-based activation.

Active Directory-Based activation uses your existing Active Directory infrastructure to activate all Office 2013 VL clients through their connection to the domain. To set up Active Directory-Based activation for Office 2013, configure Active Directory Domain Services (AD DS) from either a Windows 8 VL edition computer or a Windows Server 2012 computer. The Office 2013 VL clients can automatically activate against the domain as long as they are running on a Windows 8 or Windows Server 2012 client computer.

Source: http://technet.microsoft.com/en-us/library/dd188670.aspx#BKMK_ADBa

Apps for Office

Developers use apps for Office to create engaging new consumer and enterprise experiences that run within supported Office 2013 applications by using the power of the web and standard web technologies such as HTML5, XML, CSS3, JavaScript, and REST APIs.

An app for Office is basically a webpage that is hosted inside an Office client application. You can use apps to extend the functionality of a document, email message, meeting request, or appointment. Apps can run in multiple environments and clients. These include rich Office desktop clients, Office Web Apps, mobile browsers, and also on-premises and in the cloud. Developers can publish apps to the Office Store or to an onsite catalog, where they can be available to users from their Office 2013 applications. As the IT Administrator of your organization, you can control how the apps for Office become available to users.

Source: http://technet.microsoft.com/en-us/library/jj219429(v=office.15).aspx

Click-to-Run Customization

Administrators can customize Click-to-Run product installations. Click-to-Run for Office 365 provides a downloadable Office Deployment Tool for Click-to-Run that enables administrators to download Click-to-Run for Office 365 product and language sources to an on-premises location. This is useful in scenarios where administrators want to minimize the demand on the network or want to prevent users from installing from the Internet because of corporate security requirements.

You can download the Office Deployment Tool from the Microsoft Download Center site. The download includes a sample Configuration.xml configuration file. To customize an installation, administrators run the Office Deployment Tool and provide a customized Configuration.xml file. The Office Deployment Tool performs the tasks that are specified by using the optional properties in the Configuration.xml configuration file.

MSI and Click-to-Run installations of Office 2013 require that Task Scheduler be enabled on the client computers. If you have set up Group Policy to disable Task Scheduler, or if an individual client computer has Task Scheduler disabled, attempts to install Office 2013 will fail.

Source: http://technet.microsoft.com/en-us/library/dd188670.aspx#BKMK_
ClicktoRunCustomization

Managing Office 2013 with Group Policy

Group Policy enables administrators to apply policy settings to users and computers in an Active Directory service environment. Group Policy is the recommended tool for managing Office 2013 and Office 365 ProPlus user and computer settings that you want to enforce for both Click-to-Run and Windows Installer-based installations.

Source: http://technet.microsoft.com/en-us/library/cc179176.aspx

Office Telemetry Dashboard and Log

Office 2013 introduces a new application and document compatibility tool, known as Telemetry Dashboard. It replaces the Office 2010 compatibility tools Office Migration Planning Manager (OMPM), Office Code

Compatibility Inspector (OCCI), and Office Environment Assessment Tool (OEAT). Telemetry Dashboard helps speed up Office 2013 deployments by reducing the time needed for migration planning and compatibility assessment. IT Professionals can use Telemetry Dashboard to identify typically used Office documents and solutions in their organizations and to view application events and crash data for select Office 2013 applications.

A companion tool for Telemetry Dashboard, known as Telemetry Log, is designed for developers and expert users who want to view event data for documents and solutions as they load, run, or raise errors in Office 2013. Telemetry Log shows local event data, whereas Telemetry Dashboard combines this event data for multiple client computers.

Source: http://technet.microsoft.com/en-us/library/jj219431.aspx

Office Web Apps

When used with SharePoint 2013 on-premises, Office Web Apps provides updated versions of Word Web App, Excel Web App, PowerPoint Web App, and OneNote Web App. Users can view and, depending on the current license, edit Office documents by using a supported web browser on computers and on different mobile devices, such as Windows Phones, iPhones, and iPads.

In addition to new features in Office Web Apps, the architecture and deployment methods have also changed. Office Web Apps is no longer tightly integrated with SharePoint. Instead, it is installed separately as part of Office Web Apps Server, a stand-alone Office server product. You no longer have to optimize the SharePoint infrastructure to support Office Web Apps, and you can update servers that run Office Web Apps Server separately and at a different frequency than you update SharePoint.

Source: http://technet.microsoft.com/en-us/library/dd188670(v=office.15).aspx #bkmk_OfficeWebApps

Office Web Apps Server

Office Web Apps Server is an Office server product that provides browser-based file viewing and editing functionality for Office files. Office Web Apps Server works together with products and services that support WOPI, the

Web app Open Platform Interface protocol. These products, known as hosts, include SharePoint 2013, Lync Server 2013, and Exchange Server 2013. Here are some features that Office Web Apps Server enables for these products:

- **SharePoint 2013**   Users can access Office files from SharePoint document libraries by using Word Web App, Excel Web App, PowerPoint Web App, and OneNote Web App. There are many new features and capabilities, such as support for co-authoring in Word Web App and PowerPoint Web App.

- **Lync Server 2013**   Users can broadcast PowerPoint presentations by using Lync 2013 and Lync Web App. Broadcasting is improved to support higher-resolution displays and a wider range of mobile devices than in earlier versions. Users who have the appropriate privileges can scroll through a PowerPoint presentation independent of the presentation itself.

- **Exchange Server 2013**   In Outlook Web App, all attachments in an email are displayed in a filmstrip that includes a thumbnail of each attachment. Users can preview attachments online in full fidelity.

An Office Web Apps Server farm can provide Office services to multiple on-premises hosts. You can scale out the farm from one server to multiple servers as your organization's needs grow. Although Office Web Apps Server requires dedicated servers that run no other server applications, you can install Office Web Apps Server on virtual machine instances.

Deploying and managing Office Web Apps Server across an organization is easier now that it is a stand-alone product. You can apply updates to the Office Web Apps Server farm separately and at a different frequency than you can when you update SharePoint Server, Exchange Server, or Lync Server. Having a stand-alone Office Web Apps Server farm also means that users can view or edit Office files that are stored outside SharePoint 2013, such as those in shared folders or in document management products that support WOPI.

Source: http://technet.microsoft.com/en-us/library/jj219437.aspx

Security Changes

Several new security features make it easier for users and IT professionals to use and trust Office 2013 applications and documents. These include the following:

- **Authentication in Office**   The days are over for providing a password multiple times as users conduct normal business, opening multiple Office files from different locations. Now users create a profile, sign in one time, and can seamlessly work on and access local and cloud Office files and not be required to re-identify themselves. Users can connect multiple services such as an organization's SkyDrive or a user's personal SkyDrive account, to their Office profiles and have instant access to all files and their associated storage. Users authenticate one time for all Office applications, including SkyDrive. This is true regardless of the identity provider (Microsoft account and the user ID that you use to access Office 365) or the authentication protocol that is used by the application (for example, OAuth, forms based, claims based, or Windows Integrated Authentication). From a user perspective, it all just works. From the IT perspective, these connected services can easily be managed.

- **File password escrow key**   Office 2013 includes new functionality that lets admins unlock password-protected Office files when, for example, the file owner either forgets the password or leaves the organization. By using a new Escrow Key Admin Tool, IT personnel can easily assign a new password to the file, or no password, and can save the file to the same location or a new location. You can download the Escrow Key Admin Tool from the Connect site.

- **Digital signature**   Several digital signature improvements were made for documents created by using Office 2013 applications.

  - Users can now digitally "sign" Open Document Format (ODF v1.2) files by applying an invisible digital signature.

o Plus, Office 2013 will verify signatures on ODF files that were created by using other applications.

o XAdES digital signatures in documents that are created by using Office 2013 applications are now easier to create. XAdES signed Office 2013 documents allow signers to add their addresses, titles, and to describe the intent of their signatures. Office 2013 will also evaluate -XL signatures by using the certificates and any revocation data that is contained in the file

- **Information Rights Management** Office 2013 incorporates new Windows 2012 Active Directory Rights Management Services (AD RMS) features. Support for multiple user IDs for access to Office 365 and single sign-on makes choosing an identity and protecting content much easier for users. This new functionality and automatic service discovery eliminate the need for registry configuration.

- **Enhancements to documents opened in "protected view"** This feature, introduced in Office 2010, helps reduce exploits by opening files in a restricted sandboxed "lowbox" so it can be examined before editing. New Windows 8 capabilities mean stronger process isolation and an application container that is blocked from network access.

Source: http://technet.microsoft.com/en-us/library/dd188670.aspx#section3

Sign-in IDs

In Office 365, users can sign in by using either of two types of credentials: Personal (Microsoft account) or Organization (the Office 365 user ID that is assigned by the organization). The user enters these credentials within the user interface (UI) or they can be picked up from the operating system.

You can enable one of four sign-in states by using the **Block sign-in to Office** setting in the Registry. This setting controls whether users can provide credentials to Office 2013 by using either their Microsoft account or the Office 365 user ID assigned by the organization.

The Registry key for this setting is as follows:

HKEY_CURRENT_USER\Software\Microsoft\Office\15.0\Common\SignIn\SignInOptions

If you enable this setting, you can specify a particular sign-in option by setting one of the following values:

- 0   Both IDs allowed

- 1   Live ID only

- 2   Org ID only

- 3   None allowed

Sign-in options and their effect

If you select this...	This is what a user can do...
Both IDs allowed	Sign in and access Office content by using either ID.
Live ID only	Sign in only by using a Microsoft account.
Org ID only	Sign in only by using the Office 365 user ID that is assigned by your organization.
None allowed	Can't sign in by using either ID.

If you disable or do not configure the **Block sign-in to Office** setting, the default setting is **Both IDs allowed**. Users can sign in by using either ID.

Office 2013 automatically bootstraps itself by using any Active Directory Domain Services (AD DS) account through which the user signed in to the operating system. If that Active Directory account is federated with Office 2013, the user automatically receives all benefits of signing into Office 2013 without having to perform any additional steps.

Source: http://technet.microsoft.com/en-us/library/dd188670.aspx#BKMK_SigninIDs

Appendix 2: How to Create a .pst File in Outlook 2013

This Appendix covers the following topics:

✓   Introduction to Outlook Data Files (.pst and .ost)
✓   How to Create a .pst File in Outlook 2013

Rumors have been circulating that there is no way to create a .pst file in Outlook 2013. Those rumors are false.

The first section in this appendix is an article extracted from the Microsoft Office website explaining Outlook Data Files (.pst and .ost). The second section in this appendix shows you step-by-step how to create a .pst file in Outlook 2013.

Introduction to Outlook Data Files (.pst and .ost)

When you use Microsoft Outlook 2013, your email messages, calendar, tasks, and other items are saved on a mail server, on your computer, or both. Outlook items saved on your computer are kept in Outlook Data Files (.pst and .ost).

Outlook Data File (.pst)

The most common type of email account — a POP3 account — uses an Outlook Data File (.pst). Email messages in your POP3 account are downloaded from your mail server to the .pst file on your computer. These .pst files are saved on your computer, so they aren't subject to mailbox size limits on a mail server.   They are ideal for archiving items from any email account type. By moving items to a .pst file on your computer, you can free up storage space in the mailbox on your server. However, when messages or other Outlook items are saved in a .pst file, the items are available only on the computer where the file is saved.

Offline Outlook Data File (.ost)

Today, most email account types, other than POP3, use offline Outlook Data Files (.ost). These accounts include Microsoft Exchange Server, Microsoft Hotmail, Google Gmail, and IMAP accounts. When you use these accounts, your email messages, contacts, calendar, and other items are delivered to and saved on the server. A synchronized copy of these items are downloaded and saved on your computer in an .ost file.

When your connection to the mail server is interrupted, you still can still and compose messages. When a connection is restored, changes are automatically synchronized on the server and your computer.

File Locations

To open the folder where your Outlook Data Files (.pst and .ost) are saved, do the following:

1. In Outlook 2013, click the **File** tab.

2. Click **Account Settings**, and then click **Account Settings**.

3. On the **Data Files** tab, click an entry, and click **Open Folder Location**.

Outlook Data Files (.pst) created by using Outlook 2013 are saved on your computer in the **Documents\Outlook Files** folder. If you upgraded to Outlook 2013 on a computer that already had data files that were created in Microsoft Office Outlook 2007 or earlier, these files are saved in a hidden folder at **drive:\Users\user\AppData\Local\Microsoft\Outlook**.

The offline Outlook Data File (.ost) is saved at **drive:\Users\user\AppData\Local\Microsoft\Outlook**. There is no need to copy or back up this file because a duplicate remains on the server.

Source: http://office.microsoft.com/en-us/outlook-help/introduction-to-outlook-data-files-pst-and-ost-HA102749465.aspx

How to Create a .pst File in Outlook 2013

By default, when Outlook 2013 is installed, a new compressed version of the Outlook data file (.ost) is created to store all of your email messages, contacts, calendars, and other Outlook items. This 2013 compressed version of the .ost is up to 40% smaller than the .ost files that were created by earlier versions of Outlook.

The primary advantage of using Offline Outlook Data Files (.ost) instead of the older Personal Outlook Data Files (.pst) is that .ost files allow you to work offline when a connection to the email server is not available and then synchronize the changes when a connection is restored. For example, you can change and move items in your offline Inbox, send messages that are placed in your offline Outbox, and read your offline public folders. In the meantime, information on the server is also processing and collecting information in your absence. When a connection is restored between your local computing device and your server, the Outlook items on both are automatically synchronized. This is why the Offline Outlook Data File (.ost) is the default for Outlook 2013.

Personal Outlook Data Files (.pst) do not synchronize if changes are made while offline from the server. Many folks like this characteristic and prefer to use .pst files to archive email, contacts and calendar data on their local computer.

For example, you might create separate .pst files to archive past years of data, such as a .pst to archive your 2012 Outlook items, another .pst for 2011 Outlook items, and a third .pst to store your Outlook 2010 items.

It is not difficult to create a .pst file; however, it must be done manually and requires several steps. The following demonstration shows you how.

Demonstration – How to Create a .pst File in Outlook 2013

1. Open **Outlook 2013**.

2. Click the **File** tab and select Info.

3. Click **Accounts Settings** and select the option **Account Settings**.

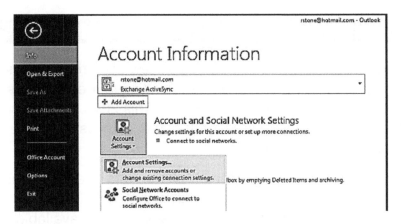

4. On the next screen, click the **Data Files** tab.

5. On the Data Files tab, click **Add**.

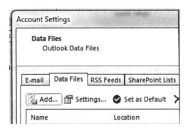

6. Save the file as an **Outlook Date File (.pst)**. Give the file a name, for example *2012 Archive.pst*, and click **OK**.

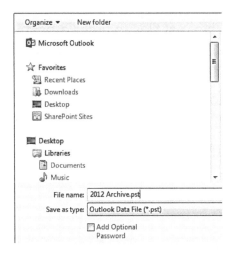

Note: Enabling the check box to add a password, does not encrypt the .pst file!

7. The new **2012 Archive.pst** file should now be listed with the path to its stored location on your computer. Click **Close**.

8. After you click **Close**, Outlook will automatically return to **Mail**. The new **2012 Archive.pst** structure will be listed in the Folder pane.

9. Right-click the top of your new **2012 Archive** structure, select **New Folder...** Name the new folder, **Inbox**. Click **OK**.

10. Now you can drag-and-drop, move or copy, old email from your current Inbox into your new 2012 Archive Inbox.

11. You're done!

Glossary

Access 2013 – A database management system from Microsoft that combines the relational Microsoft Jet Database Engine with a graphical user interface and software-development tools. The biggest enhancement to Access 2013 is web-apps, which can create SQL databases managed by a SharePoint 2013 server. Access 2013 is a member of the Microsoft Office 2013 family of applications and it is included in all Office 365 editions and the Professional traditional editions, or sold separately.

Alignment Guides – Vertical and horizontal lines in Word 2013 and PowerPoint 2013 that appear when you drag an object to the center or near the margins of the document.

App – A small application that runs in a browser or on a mobile device.

Backstage View – The area and content located under the File tab in Office 2010 and Office 2013.

Bing – An Internet search engine owned by Microsoft.

Click-to-Run – A new alternative to the traditional Windows Installer (MSI-based) method of installing and updating software. It uses Microsoft streaming and virtualization technology to download software from the cloud. If you attempt to use a software feature that is not yet installed on your local computing device, Click-to-Run will immediately download and install that feature from the cloud onto your device.

Cloud – Computing resources (hardware and software) that are delivered as a service over a network (typically the Internet). An example would be storing files on a SkyDrive, or using Hotmail for email services.

Co-Editing – Multiple users collaborating on a file stored online, typically on a SkyDrive or SharePoint server.

Enterprise – A large business or firm spread over multiple locations.

Excel 2013 – A spreadsheet application from Microsoft that combines calculation, graphing tools, pivot tables, charting, and a macro programming language based on Visual Basic. Excel 2013 is a member of the Microsoft Office 2013 family of applications, and it is included in all editions, or sold separately.

Exchange ActiveSync – A new technology that makes it possible for Outlook 2013 to synchronize calendar appointments, contacts and email from many popular online email services, such as Hotmail.

Exchange Server 2013 – An email server, calendaring software, contact and task manager developed by Microsoft. It is a server program that runs on Windows Server and is part of the Microsoft Servers line of products. The companion client component is Outlook 2013.

Eyedropper Tool – A new feature in PowerPoint 2013 used to sample colors and then apply them to text or shapes elsewhere in a presentation.

Flash Fill – A new feature in Excel 2013 that reads adjacent columns looking for similar formulas and formatting patterns so new data in a column can be automatically completed. Flash Fill can extract data, concatenate, reverse last and first names, insert letters or symbols or numbers, and repeat other patterns.

Hands-on – Learning by doing.

InfoPath 2013 – A software application for designing, distributing, filling and submitting electronic forms. In 2010, Microsoft split InfoPath into two applications: InfoPath Designer 2010 - used to create forms and define data structures; and InfoPath Filler 2010 - used to fill out and submit forms. InfoPath 2013 is a member of the Microsoft Office 2013 family of applications, and it is included in the Office 365 Small Business Premium edition and Office Professional Plus 2013 edition, or sold separately.

Inquire Tool – An add-in included in the Office Professional Plus 2013 edition that creates a new tab on the Ribbon. The tab contains tools to analyze multiple workbooks and multiple worksheets for data dependencies, formula errors, hidden information and broken links.

In-line Replies – A new feature in Outlook 2013 that allows you to Reply, Reply All or Forward from within the Mail reading pane.

Infrastructure – The technical structure composed of software and hardware that supports the computing functions of a business.

Inking – A technology on touch devices that supports writing with a finger or stylus.

JPEG or JPG – A common method of lossy compression used with digital photographs. The standard was developed by the Joint Photographic Experts Group.

Legacy – An older version, or an older standard.

Lock Tracking – A new feature in Word 2013 that prevents reviewers from accidentally turning off tracking changes. It is protected with a password.

Lync Server 2013 – A real-time communications server formerly called Microsoft Office Communications Server. Lync Server 2013 provides infrastructure for enterprise instant messaging, file transfer, peer-to-peer and multiparty voice and video calling, and web conferencing over the Internet. Lync Server 2013 also provides Lync-to-Skype Federation, support for mobile phones, and a Lync Web App. The companion client component for Lync is included in the Office 365 Small Business Premium and Office Professional Plus 2013 editions. Lync Server 2013 is included only in the Office 365 Enterprise edition.

MailTips – A dialog box in Outlook 2013 that warns you about common mistakes, such as forgetting to attach a document.

Metro – A new look for Windows 8 devices and Windows phones that uses different colored tiles to represent applications

MSI-based Installation – A traditional method of software installation that uses the Microsoft Windows Installer.

Object Zoom – A new feature in Word 2013 that allows a user to enlarge tables, charts, images, or videos, for better viewing.

Office 365 – A subscription edition of Microsoft Office which was released June 28, 2011. Support and availability is "365 days/year" because it is cloud-based. Upgrades are automatic and included in the subscription. Subscription fees vary depending on additional services included, such as Exchange Online, SharePoint Online.

Office 2013 – Read this book!

Office 365 Enterprise – A cloud-based subscription edition of Office 2013 that includes Word, Excel, PowerPoint, OneNote, Outlook, Access, Publisher, InfoPath, Lync Online, Exchange Online, SharePoint Online, and ongoing access to upgrades and multiple languages. This edition is specifically designed for large enterprises and licensed accordingly.

Office 365 Home Premium – A cloud-based subscription edition of Office 2013 that includes Word, Excel, PowerPoint, OneNote, Outlook, Access, Publisher and ongoing access to version upgrades and multiple languages. Designed for household use, this edition can be installed on up to 5 PCs or Macs, and select mobile devices such as tablets. Subscribers of this edition receive an extra 20GB of SkyDrive storage, plus 60 minutes of Skype phone calls each month to 40+ countries.

Office 365 ProPlus – A cloud-based subscription edition of Office 2013 that includes Word, Excel, PowerPoint, OneNote, Outlook, Access, Publisher, InfoPath, Lync, Exchange Online, SharePoint Online, and ongoing access to version upgrades and multiple languages. This edition is specifically designed for small to medium-sized businesses needing robust services. It allows an organization to create up to 25 user accounts. Each of these 25 users can install Office on up to 5 PCs or Macs, and on select mobile devices such as tablets.

Office 365 Small Business Premium – A cloud-based subscription edition of Office 2013 that includes Word, Excel, PowerPoint, OneNote, Outlook, Access, Publisher, InfoPath, Lync, Exchange Online, SharePoint Online, and ongoing access to version upgrades and multiple languages. Designed for small business use, this edition can be installed on up to 5 PCs or Macs, and select mobile devices such as tablets.

Office Home and Business 2013 – A desktop edition of Office 2013 that includes Word, Excel, PowerPoint, OneNote, and Outlook. It can be installed on 1 PC or Mac.

Office Home and Student 2013 – A desktop edition of Office 2013 that includes Word, Excel, PowerPoint and OneNote. It is the most basic edition of Office 2013. It can be installed on 1 PC or Mac.

Office Home & Student 2013 RT – An edition that comes pre-installed on all Windows RT devices (i.e., tablets) and includes Word, Excel, PowerPoint and OneNote optimized for the ARM processor.

Office on Demand – Streams an Office 2013 application almost instantly to a user's PC without being permanently installed on it. To get the Office on Demand benefit, a user must purchase one of the subscription editions of Office 2013. Office on Demand is available for Word, Excel, PowerPoint, Access, Publisher, Visio, and Project.

Office Professional 2013 – A desktop edition of Office 2013 that includes Word, Excel, PowerPoint, OneNote, Outlook, Access and Publisher. It can be installed on 1 PC or Mac.

Office Professional Plus 2013 – An enhanced edition of Office Professional 2013 available only from a volume-license agreement with Microsoft. This desktop edition includes Word, Excel, PowerPoint, OneNote, Outlook, Access, Publisher, InfoPath and Lync. The number of devices it can be installed on depends on the licensing agreement.

Office Web Apps – Web-based versions of Microsoft Office 2013 that allow a user to view and edit Microsoft files, which are stored online, using a web browser. Supported web browsers can be as old as Internet Explorer 7, Mozilla Firefox 3.5, Google Chrome, and Safari 4. Office Web Apps facilitate collaboration with others. Current web-apps are: Word Web App, Excel Web App, PowerPoint Web App, and OneNote Web App.

OneNote 2013 – A digital notebook from Microsoft designed for information collecting and multi-user collaboration. It can contain typed or handwritten notes, videos, screen clippings, images, drawings, and audio. These can be shared with others over the Internet. OneNote 2013 has apps for Windows Phone, iOS, Android, and Symbian, or notebooks can be accessed from a web browser using OneNote Web App. OneNote 2013 is a member of the Microsoft Office 2013 family of applications, and it is included in all editions, or sold separately.

Outlook 2013 – A personal information manager that is the preferred client for use with a Microsoft Exchange 2013 Server. Outlook organizes email, calendars, contacts and tasks. Outlook 2013 is a member of the Microsoft Office 2013 family of applications, and it is included in all editions except Office Home and Student 2013, or sold separately.

Outlook Data File (.ost) – An offline storage file for email messages, contacts, calendars and other Outlook items. It is a mirror image of the data stored on your email server, but is saved on your local computing device so you can work with Outlook items while offline. The .ost file automatically synchronizes with your email server when reconnected to it. This is the default Outlook Data File for Outlook 2013.

Outlook Data File (.pst) – A personal storage file for email messages, contacts, calendars and other Outlook items. It is saved on your local computing device. In earlier versions of Outlook, this was the default storage file for storing messages downloaded from POP3 email accounts. Newer versions of Outlook use .ost Outlook Data Files. In Outlook 2013, a .pst file must be created manually, but useful for storing archived data.

PDF Reflow – A new feature in Word 2013 that converts a .pdf file into a Word document so it can be edited.

People Card – A new feature in Outlook 2013 that merges information, obtained from multiple sources about the same person, into a single view.

Peeks – A pop-up window in Outlook 2013 and Access 2013 that allows a user to view detailed data without leaving the current view.

Power View – A reporting tool in Excel 2013 that allows a user to put tables, matrices, maps, and charts into a separate interactive view.

PowerPivot – An advanced feature in Excel 2013 that allows you to modify or build data models.

PowerPoint 2013 – An application from Microsoft that creates digital presentation slides. Slides can be created for presentation by a speaker, or run automatically from a kiosk. PowerPoint 2013 is a member of the Microsoft Office 2013 family of applications, and it is included in all editions, or sold separately.

Project 2013 – Project management software by Microsoft, which is designed to plan, assign resources to tasks, track progress, manage budgets, and analyzing workloads. Although Project 2013 is considered to be a member of the Office 2013 family of applications, it is sold separately.

Publisher 2013 – An entry-level desktop publishing application by Microsoft. The primary difference between Publisher and Word is that Publisher emphasizes page layout and design rather than text composition and proofing. Publisher 2013 is a member of the Microsoft Office 2013 family of applications. It is included in all Office 365 editions and the Professional traditional editions, or sold separately.

Quick Analysis Tool – An option box in Excel 2013 that appears when a range of data is selected. The tool contains options to apply Formatting, Charts, Totals, Tables and Sparklines.

Read Mode – A new view mode in Word 2013 that makes it easier to read Word documents on tablets and mobile devices.

Reply to Comment – A new feature in Word 2013 and PowerPoint 2013 that allows a reviewer to write a comment about a comment.

Resume Reading – A digital bookmarking technology that allows a viewer to exit an Office 2013 document, then later return to the same place, even if using a different computing device.

Ribbon – The primary user interface that replaced the menu system in Office 2007 and has existed in all versions of Microsoft Office since. The Ribbon is organized into tabs, which contain groups of related command buttons, drop-down menus, and style galleries.

Scratch Area – A workspace adjacent to the document in Publisher 2013. It is used to place imported images until they are deleted or used.

SharePoint 2013 – A management system for documents and content, developed by Microsoft. SharePoint 2013 is tightly integrated with all Office 365 editions. It can provide intranet portals, file management, collaboration, social networks, extranets, websites, enterprise search, and business intelligence. SharePoint 2013 is included in all Office 365 editions except Office 365 Home Premium, or sold separately.

Simple Markup – A new tracking option in Word 2013 that provides a cleaner look by using red-line indicators in the left margin to mark paragraphs and lines where tracked changes occurred.

Silverlight – A Microsoft software product for writing and running rich Internet applications. Silverlight has features and purposes similar to those of Adobe Flash.

SkyDrive – An online storage service hosted by Microsoft. Anyone can sign-up for a free personal SkyDrive account with 7GB storage.

Skype – On May 10, 2011 Microsoft acquired Skype Communications. Skype is a Voice over IP (VoIP) service and software application. It allows users to communicate with peers by voice using a microphone, video by webcam, and instant messaging over the Internet. Phone calls may also be placed to recipients using traditional telephone networks. Calls to other users within the Skype service are free of charge, while calls to landline telephones and mobile phones are typically charged. Lync Server 2013 now supports Lync-to-Skype. Office 365 Home Premium subscribers receive 60 minutes of Skype phone calls each month to 40+ countries.

Social Network – An online site that focuses on building social relations among people who share interests, activities, backgrounds, or real-life connections. Examples of Social Networks supported by Microsoft Office 2013 are Facebook, Twitter, LinkedIn, Flickr and Google.

SQL Azure – A cloud-based service from Microsoft that was formerly called SQL Server Data Services and later SQL Services. SQL Azure allows users to make relational queries against stored data, which can either be structured or semi-structured, or even unstructured documents. Similar to SQL Server, it uses T-SQL as the query language and Tabular Data Stream (TDS) as the protocol to access the service over internet. If you create an Access 2013 web-app on a SharePoint 2013 Server provided as part of an Office 365 subscription, the database is created in SQL Azure service residing on the SharePoint 2013 Server.

SQL Server – A robust relational database management system developed by Microsoft. It allows users to make relational queries against stored data, which can either be structured or semi-structured, or even unstructured documents. Its primary query languages are T-SQL and

ANSI SQL. If you use Access 2013 to create web-app on a SharePoint server that your company hosts, the database is created on the SQL Server designated by the SharePoint 2013 server.

Tablet – A type of mobile computing device that has a touch screen or pen-enabled interface. Microsoft began selling its first tablet, called Surface, on October 26, 2012. Two versions of Microsoft Surface are currently available: Surface RT runs the Windows RT operating system; Surface Pro runs the Windows 8 operating system.

TIFF – Tagged Image File Format. TIFF is a format used for storing images. It is commonly used by graphic artists, the publishing industry, amateur and professional photographers.

Virtualization Technology – Creates a self-contained isolated environment to run Office 2013 so it doesn't affect other applications installed on the computer. Virtualization Technology allows multiple versions of Office to run side-by-side.

Visio 2013 – A 2D-object drawing application developed by Microsoft. Although Visio 2013 is considered to be a member of the Office 2013 family of applications, it is sold separately

Visual Studio – An Integrated Development Environment (IDE) by Microsoft. It is used to develop applications, forms, web sites, and web services using common programming languages, such as C/C++, C#, F#, Visual Basic, and others.

Weather Bar – A new feature in Outlook 2013 that can be enabled in Calendars to provide a three-day forecast for any location you configure.

Windows 7 – An operating system, produced by Microsoft, for use on personal computers. Windows 7 was released to manufacturing on July 22, 2009. Windows 7 was succeeded by Windows 8 on October 26, 2012.

Windows 8 – The current release of Microsoft Windows operating system for use on computers, tablets, and phones. Windows 8 has a new user interface called "Metro", which features a grid of dynamically updating tiles to represent applications on the Start screen. Windows 8 also supports touchscreen input. Windows 8 was released on October 26, 2012.

Windows RT – a version of the Windows 8 operating system designed to run on mobile devices utilizing the ARM architecture, such as tablets.

Word 2013 – A word-processing application developed by Microsoft, which makes composition, proofing, and collaboration of documents easy. Word 2013 is a member of the Microsoft Office 2013 family of applications, and it is included in all editions, or sold separately.

WordArt – A combination of Text Fills, Text Outlines, and Text Effects found in Word 2013, PowerPoint 2013 and Publisher 2013.

Index

N

Navigation Bar, 48, 145, 146, 152, 153, 161, 163, 164, 165
Navigation Grid, 45, 126, 128, 129
New Quick Note, 148, 150, 151
newsletters, 51, 150, 172, 183

O

Object Zoom, 35, 57, 60, 65, 66, 87, 203
Office 2007, 1, 9, 12, 13, 20, 34, 35, 36, 37, 81, 82, 122, 129, 208
Office 2010, 1, 9, 12, 13, 20, 24, 34, 36, 37, 67, 81, 82, 78, 79, 112, 122, 129, 186, 188, 192, 200
Office 2011 for Mac, 2
Office 2013 Editions Compared, 6
Office 365, 2, 3, 4, 5, 6, 8, 9, 10, 11, 15, 17, 23, 53, 54, 59, 68, 79, 112, 134, 168, 170, 187, 188, 191, 192, 193, 200, 201, 202, 203, 204, 207, 208, 209
Office 365 Enterprise, 2, 8, 17, 203
Office 365 ProPlus, 2, 8, 17
Office 365 Small Business Premium, 2, 5, 6, 8, 10, 17, 53, 54, 59, 201, 202, 204
Office Deployment Tool, 187
Office Home & Student 2013 RT, 3, 9, 204
Office Home and Business 2013, 2, 4, 9, 17, 204
Office Home and Student 2013, 2, 3, 4, 9, 17, 204
Office on Demand, 5, 7, 22, 24–25, 24, 25, 56, 205
Office Professional 2013, 2, 4, 9, 17, 205
Office Store, 19, 30–32, 30, 31, 33, 56, 65, 187
Office Web Apps, 24, 149, 150, 183, 187, 189, 190, 205
Office.com, 33, 36, 43, 81, 109, 122, 123, 173
OneNote 2013, 130–52
OneNote Web App, 46, 130, 137, 141, 151, 189, 190, 205, 206
Online Email Services, 149
Online Media, 36, 60, 81, 108, 122
Online Pictures, 36, 52, 57, 61, 81, 82, 87, 108, 122, 123, 124, 129, 176

Outlook 2013, 145–66
Outlook Data Files (.pst and .ost), 193, 194
   Offline Outlook Data File (.ost), 194, 195
   Outlook Data File (.pst), 194, 206
   Personal Outlook Data File (.pst), 193
Outlook Social Connector, 156, 157, 165
Outlook.com, 147, 148, 149, 151, 165

P

PDF Reflow, 36, 57, 60, 61, 80, 206
Peek, 50, 58, 153, 165, 163, 164, 167, 168, 170
Peeks, 48, 58, 145, 146, 153, 158, 165, 206
People Card, 48, 145, 146, 158, 165, 206
Photo Printing, 52, 58, 171, 180, 181, 183
Picture Backgrounds, 52, 58, 171, 178
Picture Swap, 52, 58, 171, 177, 178, 183
PivotChart, 41, 94, 96, 97
PivotTable, 39, 40, 41, 92, 94, 96, 97
PivotTables, 40, 41, 57, 96, 106
Power View, 41, 57, 77, 78, 98, 99, 100, 101, 102, 103, 104, 106, 206
PowerPivot, 40, 41, 57, 77, 78, 100, 101, 102, 106, 207
PowerPoint 2013, 108–29
PowerPoint Web App, 30, 116, 189, 205
Prerequisites, 1–2
Presenter View, 44, 57, 108, 109, 126, 127, 128, 129
Presenting Online, 36, 57, 60, 78, 79, 87
Project, 25, 164, 165, 170, 205, 207
protected view, 192
Publisher 2013, 171–83

Q

Quick Analysis Tool, 39, 40, 57, 77, 91, 92, 93, 96, 106, 207
quick note, 148

R

Read Mode, 35, 57, 60, 61, 62, 63, 64, 65, 66, 81, 87, 207
Reading Pane, 156, 159, 165
Reading Resume, 131, 142
Recommended Charts, 40, 94, 97
Recommended PivotTables, 40

CPSIA information can be obtained at www.ICGtesting.com
Printed in the USA
LVOW02s2338100214

373176LV00004B/104/P